MW00904211

# The Big, Bad
# "B" Word

Chris "Shoof" Scheufele

ISBN: 9781086580754

To Luann, Alaina, Josiah and Lizzie.
I love you!

# CONTENTS

# ACKNOWLEDGMENTS

To Brooks Gibbs - Thank you for being a brother, friend and mentor. You taught me everything I know about this industry and I can't thank you enough for taking me under your wing and pouring into my life in so many ways.

To Jeff Veley - Thank you for being my brother, mentor, sounding board and one of my biggest encouragers. I've learned so much from you and I'm so blessed that our families are so close.

To all of my former coworkers in education - I love you all. So many of you reminded me to not "forget the little people." Please know that none of you were ever, nor will you ever be, "little people" to me. Each and every one of you encouraged, loved and supported me when things were just getting started and times were tough. I'm eternally grateful, my friends.

To all of my former students - I hope I made half the difference in your lives that you've made in mine.

# WELCOME TO THE CLASSROOM

As I reflect on over a decade in education, it's so easy to remember all of the environments I was blessed to be in. Some good. Some rough. The faces changed but the mission was always the same: Empower the next generation to be better than mine. I can honestly say that I loved every single student I encountered.

Don't get me wrong, there were plenty of students that really made me question my career choices every now and then. There were times I wasn't sure if I needed to get an administrator for disciplinary help or a priest to perform an exorcism. There were plenty of duties and responsibilities that made me wonder why I chose to do this to myself. For example, outside bus duty from December to March, or the classic teacher's definition of Hell: lunch duty in an elementary school cafeteria.

For the most part, though, each school I entered, each classroom I called home, and each student that I ever stood in front of has had an amazing impact on my life in some way, shape or form.

I was in some pretty diverse environments:

Different cities: From Baltimore, Maryland to the deserts and oil fields of western Texas, to the huge metroplex of Dallas/Fort Worth, Texas, there were substantial differences in thought processes, curricula and standards.

Schools of different sizes: One school had 80 kids combined kindergarten through 8th grade. One school had 1200 kids combined 6th through 8th grade.

Schools of different tolerances: In a few private schools, we were expected to teach religion every day. In one public school, I was reprimanded for having a sticky note of a short prayer under my computer keyboard (which stayed on my desk, in my office where no students ever went).

Schools of different economic status: One school had 85% of the students on some sort of government support program and the only meals they got were the school-provided breakfast and lunch.[1] One school had 85% of the students that came from families that made well over six figures per year (some were millionaires) and paid a very hefty tuition rate for their children to attend.

Schools in different locations: One school was in a neighborhood that was controlled by sects of the Bloods and Cryps and teachers often needed police escorts to their vehicles each day. One school was in a neighborhood surrounded by homes that were no smaller than 2,500 square feet and the only community issue they had was that a local sporting complex blocked the neighborhood view of the skyline. (How dare they!)

I don't tell you about my teaching history to brag. I don't want sympathy or empathy. Prayers? They would have been nice in some of those rougher situations. No, friends I tell you that to let you know that I have been in many different types of situations as a teacher. And, after all those experiences, I can honestly say that I've learned two things:

1. Teachers are far underpaid.
2. Dealing with kids, in any arena, is about one thing: **relationships**.

When I say that, I don't just mean relationships between adults and kids. Making sure that kids have solid relationships with

---

[1] Although, when a school serves donuts for breakfast and labels them as "Power Wheels," I'm not sure we're on the right track, nutritionally speaking.

the adults in their lives is a given. At least, I hope it is. No, I think we are dropping the ball with helping kids foster, build and cultivate proper relationships between each other. Other students. Their peers. Other people within their age range. And, I think *that's* what we need to focus on when it comes to many of the issues facing our kids every single day, including the issue of bullying.

{*Gasp!*} *He said the "B" word!*

Yup. Sure did.

Bullying is a tough topic. Think about the word "bullying." It's exploited by the media to freak people out; and it's working. Don't get me wrong, I'm not anti-media. But, I will say that the media (on both sides) does a great job of focusing on the negativity that gets people's attention. If it bleeds, it reads. The result? Parents are terrified that their children could be targets of relentless teasing and taunting. Schools are running into roadblocks and are quickly running out of ideas of exactly what to do. And, worst of all, we're all losing patience.

The traditional ways of dealing with bullying are not working. Ignore it. Walk away. Fight back. Tell an adult. We've been teaching these methods for years, but it seems that the problem keeps getting worse. In fact, things are getting so bad that kids are still being hurt and they're committing horrible acts of violence against others and themselves. Bullying is the #1 reason why kids skip school. Every day, an average of 160,000 students skip school. I recently heard a statistic that 75% of teens are cyber bullied every year but only 10% of those will tell someone and seek help. Bullying is a leading contributor to self-injurious behavior like cutting, anorexia, bulimia and suicide. There's even a new word called "bullycide," which is suicide as a result of being bullied.

Want me to keep going?

Bullying is not just a problem in the US. Today, bullying is a known problem all around the world. Europe, South America, Australia, Asia, Mexico. In fact, other countries, like Mexico, don't have an equivalent in their language for the word for bully. The closest things they have, to my knowledge, are "intimidator" and "matón." "Intimidator" generally describes someone who is, you guessed it, intimidating, which doesn't completely cover all of the needed criteria for "bullying." "Matón" is a title usually given to a street thug and is often used in the same sentence as "murderer." The majority of the time, "matón" is too strong a word to describe bullying behavior. So, other countries are using the English word "bully." They adopted our word! Doesn't that make you proud to be an American? I'm not sure, but that's not what I want other countries to adopt from us.

Are you ready? Can you handle what's coming? Parents, this book is for you, and I don't plan to hold back. I don't plan to be politically correct. I plan to be honest. I plan to be open. I plan to tell you wholeheartedly what I have seen work and fail in the world of students, social aggression and bullying.

I'll tell you about the shortcomings of many school systems across the country, but I'll also point out the shortcomings of many parents across the country. Some things might sting a little. Some things may be eye opening. Some things may tick you off. Some things may have you sitting back in your seat saying, "I've never thought of it *that* way before!"

Most of all, I want to do one better than most anti-bully programs out there. I want to offer *real* solutions that you can implement with your kids right away, along with the knowledge of why they work; not just the same old shtick we hear from many (but not all) of the schools. In other words, I want to offer you time-tested, psychologically-proven ways that you can **bully-proof** your kids at home so they can go throughout their school careers, and the rest of their lives, with the knowledge of what's ahead and the skills and resources to conquer whatever comes their way.

Some of you may not like me very much throughout this book. You may get angry in some spots. But it's ok. I'm not on this mission to win friends. I'm on this mission because the truth needs to be heard. I look at things from a psychological perspective, and I love it because psychology doesn't worry about feelings and emotions. Psychology is about researched, time-tested facts. The famed, late psychiatrist Elisabeth Kubler-Ross said, "The truth does not need to be defended." While I wholeheartedly agree, I will say that the truth *does* need a voice. If the truth upsets you, please understand the fact that it is my goal to communicate the truth out of love.

Whatever the case, please understand this one thing: we're on the same side. We all want the best for our kids. Emotionally, physically, and educationally.

Before we start this journey, I want every adult to know this one thing. When a kid comes to you seeking help with a social problem such as bullying, remember this: they came to *you*. They didn't go to another counselor, another teacher, another administrator, another adult. They came to you. Do you know what that means? They came to *you* for a reason. They trust *you*. They trust that *you* can help them with their problem. So, consider how it would look to that child if you send them to someone else with whom they don't have as close of a relationship. Or, how it would look if you gave them the same old faulty advice that has been failing for years. This is why every parent, every teacher, every adult needs to understand the things in this book.

I'm a veteran teacher. I'm a son. I'm a father. I'm a husband. I'm an uncle. Trust me when I say that I have experienced, witnessed, researched, taught and implemented everything I'm about to tell you. My heart is for the next generation. Friends, they are our legacy. Let's empower them to, not just carry our torch, but make the flame even brighter than ours!

PART 1: SAME OLD, SAME OLD

# HEY! LANGUAGE!

Have you ever had one of those words that you couldn't stand? I mean, the mere utterance of the word makes your skin crawl? Seeing it written makes you want to scream? For many people, "moist" is that word. For many, the word "moist" is just as cringeworthy as fingernails on a chalkboard. I have many friends that wish it would be done away with. I have a very similar issue with the words associated with bullying.

Let's start with the word "bullying" itself. Yes, I'm the bullying-prevention guy. Yes, I make my living by helping students, parents and teachers overcome bullying issues. Yes, I realize I have to hear it and say it and live with it. But, it's turned into one of *those* words. It's turned into one of those words that makes people (particularly school admin and counselors) roll their eyes in exhaustion and frustration. Personally, I think we need to get rid of the word. "Bullying" is now a catch-all term for any mean behavior. Literally, *any* mean behavior. School counselors and administrators have been bombarded by phone calls and emails from angry parents saying that their student is being "bullied" and it needs to be stopped.

Anytime I speak with a teacher, counselor, principal, parent or student about such an issue, I'm very frank. Right up front I say, "Don't tell me your child is being bullied. Tell me specifically what happened." Now, when I say this to a room full of school employees, they nod wildly in agreement. One time, I even got a standing ovation…which was odd because I had only been on the stage for 5 minutes.

Don't tell me your child is being bullied. Tell me *specifically* what is going on. Name calling? I can help. Pushing and shoving? I can help. Rumors? I can help. Mean jokes? I can help. Social exclusion? I can help. Cyber nonsense? I can help. But please, be specific and tell me what exact behavior is taking place.

"But Chris, 'bullying' is such a convenient word that helps us encompass so many types of mean behavior into a simple package." Agreed. But, as you'll see in a bit, it's not helping anything. In fact, the word is causing more harm than good. According to the American Psychological Association, bullying is aggressive behavior.[2] Of course there are many types of aggression - verbal, physical, direct, indirect, etc. - but suffice it to say that bullying is aggression. It's a better fit for what is actually taking place. Don't be shocked if I purposefully switch back and forth between the two words from here on. I think you'll come to understand why.

## *I Saw the Sign*

Another thing that gets me fired up in this instance is the use of posters in schools. Hallways and classrooms in nearly every school across the country are covered with signs and posters opposing and denouncing bullying. "Stop Bullying!" "Don't Be a Bully!" "Bullies aren't cool. Kick them out of school."[3] Those are just a few of the things that are lining the walls of schools everywhere. And, why not? They come from a good place with good intentions. But, let's look at this from another angle.

Imagine for a moment that you are trying to stop your children from using foul language. What would you do? Would you just tell them to stop and allow them to hang out with the same people and to continue watching and engaging in all of the programming and media as they normally do? I sure hope not. I'd hope you would dig deep and delve into all of the language outlets

---

[2] https://www.apa.org/topics/bullying/

[3] Yes, that's was on an actual poster I saw in one school.

that were entering your child's ears, and remove the sources of the inappropriate language so they don't even have the slightest temptation towards it anymore.

I ask you that to ask you this: By having all of those posters on the wall, visible, at all times of the day, what words are the students seeing over and over and over and over again?  Answer: Bully, bullying, bullies, bully, bully, bully…. (Especially when the word is usually highlighted, underlined, enlarged or colored differently than the rest of the text on the poster.)  Psychologically speaking, they are being bombarded with the very word we are trying to eliminate!  Yet we are surprised that, despite all the posters and signs, the problem isn't going away!

The first step to stopping bullying: **STOP USING THE WORD!**

### *You Don't Know Me*

Until recently, it was widely accepted that a bullying situation had 3 main players with no questions asked:

> **The Bully:** The bad guy.
> **The Victim:** The innocent target and recipient of the mean behavior.
> **Bystander:** Anyone that witnesses the mean behavior.  If they speak up and try to stop the behavior, they are heroes.  If they don't, they are just as guilty as the bully.  (We'll talk about bystanders later.)

I'm about to say something I don't say very often.  Something crazy.  Something out there.

{Deep breath.}  {Center self.}

The government is right about something.  {GASP!}

Now before you freak out, hear me out.  In 2017, the officials at the U.S. Department of Health and Human Services updated some of their content regarding the parties involved in a "bullying" situation.  They claim that, according to their research, using labels and language like "bully," "victim," and "bystander" are harmful to aggressive situations and may have unintended consequences. They say that labeling kids can imply that the child cannot change, ignore the fact that a student can play multiple different roles in any given situation, and disregard the fact that many conflicts run incredibly deep and have a convoluted back story with many layers.[4]

While I'm happy to give credit where credit is due, the government is slightly behind the times on this one - although I'm glad they're catching up. In 2013, clinical psychologist Dr. Susan Eva Porter wrote a great deal in her book, *Bully Nation,* about the troubles with assigning labels to students in "bullying" situations. You'll never guess what she said. Ok, maybe you will. She said the exact... same...things. Dr. Porter also asserts that, although it simplifies the situation, thinking of children as bullies, victims and bystanders automatically creates a fixed, one-sided, one-way street that follows the "guilty until proven innocent" mentality. Those labels define a child's character, sometimes falsely, rather than describe a specific behavior.[5]

I've heard people say, "Once a bully always a bully." That's ridiculous, especially for kids. From all of my years in the classroom, I've seen some of the biggest elementary school problem children grow and change into the sweetest, kindest high school graduates. When you have a fixed mindset about a child's character, you are putting them into a box and telling them there is no way to escape, when in reality, there are plenty of chances and opportunities throughout childhood and adolescence to change and grow out of specific behavior.

The same goes for victims. Psychology has shown that when kids believe they are victims, they have a higher tendency to have a long-lasting victimization mindset. They feel entitled to hold onto the pain, which is emotionally unhealthy. If the goal is to have an emotionally healthy and resilient child, it is counterproductive to allow them to have the mindset of a victim. Using labels such as "bully" and "victim" will only perpetuate those negative mindsets and create an uphill, nearly impossible situation for growth.

---

[4] https://www.stopbullying.gov/what-is-bullying/roles-kids-play/index.html

[5] Porter, Susan Eva. *Bully Nation.* Paragon House 2013. p. 23.

Nationally renown social skills educator and speaker Brooks Gibbs says that when the word "bully" is being used, common sense and logic are usually not. The least effective way to solve a conflict is to keep using the language that perpetuates it. What if, instead of referring to kids as "bullies" and "victims," we refer to them as...wait for it...kids?

# WUDDYA MEAN?

We've all had those moments where we've said something like, "If I had a nickel every time I've had to tell my kids to stop fighting, I'd be rich." Or, "If I had a dollar for every time I had to remind my son to use soap in the shower, I'd never have to work again." That'd sure be nice. The money part, that is.

Here's a new one: If I had a dollar for every time I've heard or read somebody twist and distort the true definition of "bullying," I'd be able to:

1. Buy a private island.
2. Buy a private jet.
3. Hire a private pilot.
4. Have said private pilot fly me and my family on said private jet to said private island and enjoy the characteristic "Hakuna Matata Jimmy Buffet" lifestyle for the rest of my life.

Think about the words "bully" and "bullying." The news is filled with story after story of kids who just want to learn and go through their day free of worry and pain, but instead they are faced with the torment, name-calling, shaming and exclusion that seems to be invading our schools at an epidemic rate.

Schools are confused as to what to do. In fact, not only are they confused, but they are scared! I have talked to so many counselors, principals and superintendents who have told me that one of the biggest fears of a school, and the surrounding community, is that they will end up on the evening news and have the entire nation see them in a negative light because they "cannot control the school's bullying problems."

Parents are afraid to let their kids go to school every day because they fear what mental and emotional harm could be waiting for them at one of the very places that is supposed to be a beacon of safety and security. In addition, parents are furious. They want to know how schools can let these things happen to their kids. Parents place their trust in the schools to educate and protect their children every day. How's that working? For the most part, I'd say ok. But, in some cases, as we all know, some parents are finding their hopes unfulfilled and that trust betrayed. Who gets the blame? The school, of course.

So, let's take a closer look at the actual word "bully" so we can get a good idea of how to frame, and ultimately solve, the problem.

### *History Lesson*

This will blow your mind! The word "bully" was first used in the 1500's by the Dutch. Guess what it originally meant! *Best friend. Loved one.* Crazy, right? It's true. If I wanted to introduce my best friend, I'd say, "This is my bully, Jason." Similarly, if I wanted to introduce my significant other, I would, very sappily and with puppy dog eyes, say, "This is my sweetheart, my bully." When I speak to live audiences, I always make the joke that the people used to gaze into each other's eyes with all that lovey-dovey stuff and say, "I bully you." And, the other would blushingly reply, "I bully you, too." In fact, my wife and I made a vow to "bully" each other for the rest of our lives.[6]

Anyway, the definition of the word stayed that way for a couple hundred years.

Fast forward to the 1700's. "Bully" was brought to the United States and its definition expanded a little. People started to

---

[6] That is…in the original Dutch, lovey-dovey sense of the word.

use it as a term to mean anything good.  They would say, "Bully!" and "Bully for you!"  It meant, "Awesome!  Good for you!  Way to go!"  And, again, it stayed that way for a couple hundred years.

Fast forward, again, to the early 1900's.  President Teddy Roosevelt began to use the word "bully" in almost every speech.  It became the lingo of that day.  He would fire up the crowd and say, "Bully!"  And the people would respond, "Bully!"  In fact, he labeled the White House a "bully pulpit."[7]  In Roosevelt's words, it meant that he wanted the White House to be the biggest platform in the world to do the most good.  Quite noble.

So, you're probably wondering, like many when I tell this story, "What the heck happened?"  If it meant so many good things for hundreds of years, how did the word "bully" become so vicious, venomous and vile?  If it was such a positive word and sparked so much good, how did it transform to mean things like "hater", "jerk", "punk" and "meanie"?  (And in some cases these days, "criminal.")

Fast forward one more time to the year 1970.  A researcher from Norway named Dan Olweus (pronounced Ol-vay-us) was commissioned by his government to research social conflict among children in schools.  You'll never guess what he found.  Name-calling.  Pushing and shoving.  Social exclusion.  Rumors.  Teasing.  Mean jokes.

{*Gasp!*}  Wait a minute!  Those sound like everyday, immature, aggressive, child-like behaviors that have happened on school playgrounds for decades.  If you're anything like me, you're probably wondering, "What was so ground-breaking about that?"  Sounds like Norway wasted money.  (But, honestly, when hasn't a government ever spent money to learn things we already knew?)  I digress.

Most of you know exactly what I'm talking about.  Parents, remember when we were kids?  There was no "bullying" as we know it today.  It was just kids picking on each other.  Kids being punks or jerks.  I'm willing to bet that every person has a story of the

---

[7] I'm sure many of you are thinking, "The White House is still a bully pulpit."  I don't mean it in *that* way.

playground bully, the cafeteria punk, or the gym tough guy that would try to push people around and exert dominance over everyone else. It was just the mean kid on the playground that pushed kids around. It was a mean girl who spread rumors. It was the jerk in the locker room who snapped people with towels. It was the inconsiderate punk who made up a chant or song about kids to make them cry.

Olweus wanted to use one word to encompass all of his findings: both direct conflict (pushing and shoving and name-calling), but also indirect conflict (rumors, gossip and social exclusion). Some accounts say he wanted to use the word "mobbing" to describe the behavior he was seeing because he was influenced by other researchers who were studying the behavior of chickens. (Hang on, I'm connecting the dots.)

My wife grew up on a farm in Nebraska, so I've seen this first hand. Chickens will often have a pecking order; a hierarchy. If there is a weak or smaller chicken, the rest of the group will often gang up on it and peck it to death or exclude it so it will starve and die of malnutrition. But, according to the story, Dan Olweus didn't like the word "mobbing" because true mobbing was always done by a group of chickens, hence the word "mob." On the contrary, the majority of the time, he observed one-on-one conflict between students. So, he decided to pick the word "bullying," and by doing so, forever changed the word.

Almost 30 years later, April 20,1999 to be exact, the shooting at Columbine High School in Littleton, Colorado spawned the birth of the anti-bullying movement as we know it today. Many reports point to the fact that Eric Harris and Dylan Klebold were victims of bullying and mistreatment from their peers. From there, the national uproar became all about the anti-bully movement. Consequently, the only research that was ever done by a legitimate researcher was that of Dan Olweus.

### *So, what is bullying?*

In his research, Dan Olweus, who is now known as the father of the modern day anti-bullying movement, told us that there are three things that have to be present to define behavior as "bullying." These definitions are in almost every state law, every policy and every anti-bullying training in the country. (Trust me, I've looked at a ton of them.)

1. Imbalance of power.
2. Intent to cause harm.
3. Repetition over time.

Let's break these down a bit.

First, the most basic part of the bullying definition is that there is an imbalance of power. One person is more powerful than another. Please note, this doesn't necessarily mean size or strength. Of course, we all visualize the giant stereotypical linebacker picking on the skinny nerdy kid. It very well could be that. However, it could also be a tiny, innocent-looking cheerleader making the big, bad linebacker bend, break and succumb to her will. Size, strength and age have very little to do with power imbalances. The majority of the time, as we'll see later, the imbalance is actually mental and/or emotional. Regardless, one person is exercising power over someone else; the power to drive them crazy. The power to get some type of reaction out of them. Or, as I tell student audiences, simply the power to make others upset.

Second, there is an intent. Whether the behavior is direct or indirect, physical or verbal, it cannot be a mindless accident. According to Olweus, the aggressor deliberately performs the behavior in order to accomplish a goal – to establish or reinforce an imbalance of power over another. They are hoping to incite a reaction of some sort, which, in turn, makes the aggressor feel powerful.

The third part of the Olweus bullying definition is that the behavior is repeated over time. They do it over and over and over again. Whether it's hurt feelings, a diminished social status, anger, or tears, any type of reaction to the initial behavior will keep the aggressor coming back for more. They love it. They feed off of it. It feeds that innate psychological desire for dominance, and, almost instinctually, they will continue to do it.

Parents, you are bullied by your own kids. Don't believe me? Has this ever happened? Imagine a toddler at dinner. This angelic, smiling child is beaming with excitement because you just presented them with their very own bowl of spaghetti. Now, veteran parents know that it doesn't take a rocket scientist to realize that no bib, no towel, no hazmat suit will protect that precious child's face and clothes (or the kitchen floor) from what is about to take place. Rookie parents…well…at least they get an A for effort. It starts with a smear of sauce across the lips. Then it makes its way to the chin and cheeks. Before you know it, your child is laughing hysterically and you are trying to figure out how in the world spaghetti sauce made it into their hair and where they learned to pull a noodle through their nose and out of their mouth.

What do the parents do? "Stop that right now! Sit up straight! Get the food in your mouth! Quit making such a mess!" All the while, the child is laughing, performing balancing acts with the bowl and attempting to set the distance world record for spaghetti flinging.

Is your heart racing right now? Are you sweating? If so, you're probably reliving that experience as it played out at your table. That adorable, little, spaghetti sauce-covered toddler has power over you: the power to drive you crazy, and because of your reaction, they continue to laugh and make a bigger mess. No, I'm not calling your child a bully. I'm using the scenario as a real life example of how these criteria can work in almost any setting.

### The Cycle of Aggression

Here's an easier way to look at it. I call it "The Cycle of Aggression."

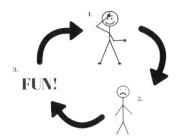

Step 1, a mean person mistreats someone else. Step 2, the target gets upset. Step 3, because the target gets upset, the mean person sees their tactics working, they feel power, they have fun, and they do it again. Around and around and around the cycle. Often times, with each trip around the cycle, things intensify, the aggression gets worse, the target gets more upset and the mean person, ultimately, gets more enjoyment out of it.

### *Wait a second!*

When some people hear this they inevitably jump to conclusions (and their feet) and think, "This sounds like a sociopath! They are someone who enjoys inflicting pain on someone weaker than themselves." And the funny thing is, that's one of the biggest misconceptions that the media wants us to believe. They want us to think that anyone labeled a "bully" has sociopathic tendencies. And some people, when they hear this, will automatically hop on the bandwagon and say, "Yup, that kid that's picking on my kid is a sociopath! Complete psycho!" Hmm, calm down Mama Bear. Probably not. In reality, only around 1% of people are sociopathic and are typically locked up in mental facilities or prison.

Besides, Dan Olweus didn't observe sociopathic behavior in his research. What did he observe? Human nature. Kids being kids. He did not see some psychological disorder at work. Just kids being kids.

You see, the definition of "bullying" does not, and should not, include things that cause objective harm. Objective harm includes anything that can harm your body or property. We have laws against those things. It does not include one kid punching another kid in the face. No, that's assault and battery. There are laws against those things. They are crimes. The definition of "bullying" does not include taking someone else's things. That's called theft. There's a law against that. It's a crime. Bullying is not breaking someone's things. That's called vandalism or destruction of property. There's a law against that. It's a crime. All those things cause *objective* harm. The harm is done to body or property.

"Bullying," in its true definition, is only about things that cause *subjective* harm; meaning that the pain is only subject to what you feel about it. So, really, "bullying" is only about noncriminal behaviors that hurt someone's feelings. In my opinion, Olweus picked the wrong word. If you thesaurus the word "bully," it just means "jerk," "meanie," "teaser" or "annoyer." But, now we've *given* it a sociopathic definition, and we've *turned it into* a psychological disorder. However, there's one problem. There's no test that a psychologist can perform to determine whether or not someone is a bully. It's not a diagnosis. The only way to tell if a kid is a "bully," by its clinical definition, is if they did or said something to someone else that hurt their feelings over and over again with the intent of causing harm.[8]

But, it's a complicated problem. It's a very complicated problem. There are so many types of aggressive behaviors that we hear about that are considered "bullying": verbal, physical, social, and cyber. Within each of these types are many facets of examples. According to most accepted definitions, verbal bullying can include things like name-calling, teasing, taunting, slurs and insults. Physical bullying can include things like pushing, shoving, pinching, flicking and tripping.[9] Social bullying can include things like exclusion from a group, rumors and attempting to damage a reputation. Cyber bullying is generally the same as verbal and social, just done online through messages and apps.[10]

Let me ask you: have you ever called someone a name? Have you ever spread a rumor about someone or perpetuated negative gossip? Have you ever purposely excluded someone? Have you ever flicked, pushed, punched or tripped someone just to agitate them? Have you ever intentionally done something to get under someone else's skin and then laughed about it because in some weird way it made you feel good or gave you an upper hand over them?[11] I'm willing to bet that we all have done at least one of those things at some point in our lives. So, by definition, we are *all* bullies!

---

[8] And of course I'm going to rip that apart later. Stay tuned.

[9] A word about physical bullying: There is a fine line between physical bullying and assault. The general rule of thinking is that physical bullying does not cause extreme pain, bruises or injury requiring medical attention.

[10] Generally, the spreading of nude, pornographic or indecent pictures is not bullying and violates many laws. If this is happening, please consult the authorities.

[11] These are meant to be rhetorical questions.

Ok, ok. I'll come back to Earth.

Friends, the word "bullying" as we understand it today may be fairly new, but the truth is that the concept of social aggression, and the types of behaviors and conflicts that are lumped into the definition of bullying, have been around since the beginning of human existence. By using the traditional definition of "bullying," we're essentially equating a large population of kids to evil, psychotic, sociopathic criminals, which is hugely inaccurate.

## *Going Out on a Limb*

Keeping everything in mind that we've covered so far, I'm going to take it one more step. Many schools, districts and companies are incredibly bent on ending bullying by stopping mean behavior – *only*. They have posters, signs and scrolling website banners that boast about how they prohibit bullying. P-r-o-h-i-b-i-t. (Some of you already see where I'm going with this.)

I think one lesson that is missing from many homes, families and schools is this simple truth: there have always been, and will always be mean people. Not everyone is going to like you. Not everyone is going to be your friend. There have always been and will always be people who push, shove, spread rumors, call names, exclude others from their groups, and make fun of others. For thousands of years, people have been trying to make peace and harmony and it has not happened. Why? Not because their efforts aren't good enough. Not because they're missing some secret ingredient. It's simply because there has always been, and will always be, people who say and do mean things.

When I speak to students, I make sure they are well aware of that fact. Not so they give up hope. Not to downplay the movements of peace. They are vital for expanding and prolonging the kindness and peace that still exist. I teach it so they understand that things will never be 100% peaceful. Why? Simple. Psychology has proven that people who hurt others are typically hurting on the inside. Hurting people hurt other people. And there are a lot of hurting people in the world. As a society, we can get better at spreading peace and kindness; don't get me wrong. But, completely eradicating mean behavior is impossible no matter how many signs, banners, posters or authority figures there are.[12]

Schools can prohibit mean behavior all they want. Is that really going to put an end to it? Is it really going to make a mean kid stop for a second and say to himself, "Oh wait! My school doesn't allow this. Maybe I should stop." Doubtful. If that were the case, kids wouldn't run in the halls. They would get to class on time. They wouldn't cuss. They would be in dress code. Schools wouldn't need consequences to go with their rules and laws. We could be, as Aristotle said, a self-policing society. But I can tell you from years of experience with children, that a policy, a sign, a prohibition does not always stop a behavior.

Kids are smart. They can be sneaky. They find ways to get away with things. Come on, parents. You remember what it's like to be a kid. How many prohibited things did you get away with? What did you do that *your* parents and teachers never found out about? (Given the fact that my parents will likely read this book, I won't share any personal examples.[13]) However, suffice it to say that kids will always find ways to get around the rules. If a kid is going to "bully" another kid, they'll find ways to do it. They'll find a time, a place, a volume, a tone, a method…. They will figure it out. Kids will be kids.

As you'll see in the coming chapters, the key to stopping aggressive behavior is not to put all of our eggs in the "just be kind to everybody" basket. While I completely support the kindness movements taking place in schools all across the country, that is only one side of the equation. This is a multi-faceted battle. It's time to open our eyes to what's been missing, despite it being right under our noses all along.

---

[12] If you're a religious person, that is until you get to heaven.

[13] Love you, Mom and Dad!

# LAW AND ORDER

{Scene} *Evening news on TV. A female news anchor turns to the camera with a serious look on her face; almost frowning. A square image appears over her left shoulder with a cartoon picture of a big, bald kid (with a tattoo and ear ring) punching a small, stereotypical nerd kid. Across the bottom of the picture in a terrifying font is the word* "BULLYING!" *Across the bottom of the TV screen is a footer that reads,* "Local Bullied Student Goes Viral".

(I know you know how the rest of the story plays out, but just for fun, let's keep going.)

*Anchor:* Bullying continues to plague schools all across the country and one student at Johnson Middle School is making headlines with his story. Field reporter Mike Rofone has more on this story.

{*Fade to a blurry shot of a school hallway with students walking by laughing, talking and waving at the camera.*}

*Mike Rofone Voice Over:* It seemed like just another day at Johnson Middle School. Busy hallways, loads of homework and lunches not even fit for a junkyard dog. Except for one student, Tyler Murphy. {*On screen: Tyler's recent school picture. He is round-faced, wears glasses, appears to be a bit stout, and has shaggy brown hair.*} In the latest video to go viral, Tyler and his mom Kimberly, describe, in detail, the torment he's been dealing with that all came to a head last Wednesday.

22

{*Cut to shaky cell phone video of Tyler and Kimberly sitting in the car after school. Tyler looks as if he's been crying. Kimberly has an angry look on her face that could derail a freight train.*}

*Kimberly*: What did he say to you? What did that jerk do to you?

*Tyler*: He said I was fat and that I needed two chairs to sit at the lunch table. And then he started making pig noises.

*Kimberly*: Why the {*beep*} did he do that?!

*Tyler*: I don't know, Mom! I just want him to stop!

*Kimberly*: How long has this been going on?

*Tyler:* {*Through tears*} Every day since school started.

*Kimberly*: Have you told anyone? Did you tell a teacher or the principal?

*Tyler*: Yeah, I told the principal, guidance counselor, teachers, friends…Nobody did anything!

{*Cut to Mike Rofone standing outside of the school, in front of the school's sign.*}

{*Awkward pause as Mike Rofone is staring at the camera waiting for his cue to begin speaking.*}

*Mike Rofone*: Now, we did ask the school administration for further details on this story and they issued a statement saying:

> *We have an anti-bullying policy in place in accordance with district and state guidelines. We are conducting an investigation and hope to uncover more details over the coming days. Johnson Middle School does not tolerate bullying of any kind and will continue to review its anti-bullying policy and uphold all aspects of it.*

As for Tyler Murphy, it is unknown whether he will return to Johnson Middle School or if his mother will move him to another school for the remainder of the year. No word on any of the alleged bullies at this time. At Johnson Middle School, I'm Mike Rofone, Channel 13 News. Back to you in the newsroom.

*Anchor:* Thank you, Mike. Up next, a look at the weather and it may not be the greatest if you're planning on heading to the big game this weekend. Meteorologist Ty Foon has your weekend forecast right after this.

{*End Scene*}

How many stories have we seen and heard over the last few years that appear exactly like that? Kid gets bullied. Story goes viral. Story makes the news. School issues the same old statement. It's like they all have a copy of it saved on the computer desktop, change the names and date, copy, paste, attach, send, and then, "Whew! We're covered."

But, are they? Are they really covered? Or, is it just smoke and mirrors to bide time until the story blows over and they can just go back to business as usual – out of the public eye? We don't know for sure, but I've talked with dozens of parents that are calling the schools' bluff and refusing to fall for a head fake anymore. They are starting to hold schools accountable.

## *A Brief Analysis*

I'm a "words" person. I look at the words that people use for things and I read deeply into them. So, when a school or district issues a statement that sounds similar to the fabricated example used here, I tend to raise an eyebrow and dig a little deeper; as I think we all should. Let's break it down.

> *We have an anti-bullying policy in place in accordance with district and state guidelines.*

Ok, great. Every state has laws and guidelines in place that require all schools to have a bullying policy of some sort. Many states don't say exactly what those policies must say or do because there are so many routes to take. But, the main point is that it is required that each school has some sort of policy in place.

24

*We are conducting an investigation and hope to uncover more details over the coming days.*

Unless the school has cameras in every orifice of the building, including audio recording (which is illegal without permission from 100% of the people involved), the investigation will include interviews with the target, the alleged "bullies" and witnesses. You can imagine the result of interviewing several children to try and get to the bottom of a situation. (I'll talk more about this part later. It's a hot button.)

> *{Insert School Name} does not tolerate bullying of any kind and will continue to review its anti-bullying policy and uphold all aspects of it.*

At the risk of sounding rude and snide (although I'm really not trying to), I have a few questions.

1. *"Continue?"* Were they actively reviewing the bullying policy to begin with? (Answer: Probably not.)

2. While I'm sure they will continue to uphold all of the policy's aspects, how did that work for them in deterring *this* situation? (Rhetorical)

3. What aspects of the current policy will prevent future situations from arising? (Answer: Likely none.)

4. How does the current bullying policy and its aspects help the targeted student? (My favorite. Answer: It probably doesn't.)

## *Diving In*

Want to know a fun fact? Consider this: There are currently more anti-bullying programs and policies in the United States than ever before. Fact. So, it would stand to reason that since there are so many policies and programs, the problem should be diminishing. That would make sense. But, as you probably guessed, it's quite the opposite. The truth is that schools that have strict anti-bullying policies tend to have the highest "bullying" numbers. So, now just what do these programs and policies say? Let's dive in and take a look.

**Note: Please keep in mind, I'm taking a very macro, global look at some common themes that occur throughout a majority of anti-bullying policies around the country. This is in no way reflective of EVERY school.**

School anti-bullying policies usually start out with a definition, obviously. They have to give a basis for what they are talking about. Be aware, some will outline things like assault, vandalism and sexual offenses as "bullying." While they *can* be used in bullying fashion, those behaviors in and of themselves are crimes and should be treated as such. Many will attempt to marry the definitions of bullying and harassment. Be careful. Most state harassment laws require that the behavior cause a credible threat to a person's safety, ability to escape the situation, liberties and rights. This is completely separate and should not be included in the same definition as "bullying."

Afterwards, the policy will usually go on to explain the consequences for a student found guilty of bullying, followed by a few resources in place for anonymous reporting and the contact information for the school counselor. And…that's about it. Where's the meat and potatoes of the policy? Usually in the consequences. Don't believe me? I'd encourage you to read the bullying policy of your child's school district. Read it carefully. Does it talk mainly of punishments and consequences for the "bully?" I'd bet it does. Does it offer any concrete resources and solutions for targets? I'm guessing not. Oh sure, there may be some links and websites to visit, but the majority of the websites speak only about telling an adult, defining behavior, how to engage in conversations and how to raise awareness. Well, guess what. We're aware! We've been aware! No solid prevention strategies for targets. No empowerment.

To make matters worse, some of the typical anti-bully programs boast about a 20% success rate. Now, I'm no Einstein, but to me, 20% success sounds more like 80% failure. As a teacher, if I gave a student a 20% on an assignment, I doubt they would call that "successful."

## Law vs. Psychology

Many anti-bully programs and activists invoke fear. They play on the horrific nature and disastrous events that happen as a result of bullying. They exploit the violence, emotional turmoil and community detriment to urge lawmakers to implement more laws and policies to advance their agenda. They say we need more reporting, more policing, more legislation and more laws. They want to take a legal approach to what is actually just a *social* problem. I'm not downplaying any of those types of events that occur because someone was mistreated and pushed past their mental and emotional limit. Mental illnesses, assaults, homicides, mass shootings and suicides are very serious and their impact should not be diminished. But, when you try to solve a social problem, such as "bullying," with a legal route, things get even more complicated, and nobody really wins. It just makes things worse.

In fact, the very nature of a lawyer, legislator, and the majority of the anti-bully movement, is that the targets are, either by nature or education, powerless and unable to solve their own social problems. Re-read that sentence. That's pretty insulting, if you ask me. But, that's how lawyers work. That's how they make money. They see a problem and then find a law, write a law or make a law to change the world around the target. Their goal is, essentially, to force everyone, everywhere, to be nice and polite to the target.

NEWS FLASH! That's just not possible. Not only is it impossible, but it does not help the target at all. It doesn't solve the root of the issue. At best, it puts a temporary bandage on the situation in hopes of eventual healing. It keeps the target in the same state and gives them the false illusion that the world is going to change to accommodate them. This is exactly what is happening with the helicopter and lawnmower parent mindset. It does more harm than good.

The problem is, friends, we can't make a law that gets someone in trouble for just hurting someone else's feelings. We can't make a law that forces everyone to be nice to everyone. Society wouldn't be able to function if we got into a legal battle every time someone's feelings got hurt. "You upset me when you said that. I'm going to sue the pants off you." What would that do? If you think

27

about it, this would actually take away freedom of speech. And we can't do that.

"But they don't have a right to say things like that! They don't have a right to hurt my child's feelings!" Actually, they do. I'm not saying it's right. I'm not saying it's moral. I'm not saying it's polite. But, because of the Constitution, and the laws of this country, they have every bit of a right, *just like you do*, to say what they want to whomever they want. We can't make a law that says everybody has to be nice to everybody. You can't police that. You can't enforce that. Now, it *is* unlawful to scream "FIRE" in a crowded room or incite violence. But, when you think you have the right that everyone must be nice to you, you are setting yourself up for failure. You are actually hurting yourself. You are giving yourself, and your child, a victim mentality. People *do* have a right to say those things to you and your child. It's called the First Amendment right of free speech; even if what they say is wrong or hateful. Our country was founded and built on the principle that everyone has the right to think and speak their mind, even if it offends other people, and that is so important to the development of the humanity and civility of this country. {Stepping down off my soapbox.}

The whole "punish the bully" mentality is faulty. Most people think it will teach them a lesson, and they will change after receiving a consequence. In reality, though, numerous psychological studies have shown that the majority of the kids that are labeled as "bullies" actually feel like victims first in another, possibly unrelated, situation. Whether it's from another student, a parent, or another adult, most "bullies" feel like victims. So, they feel the need to do something to minimize their own victimization; like picking on another kid. Since they already feel like a victim, and then get punished for how they handle their victimization, that just adds fuel to the fire. It's a recipe for disaster that will result in more acting out. We'll get into this more in a later chapter.

Don't get me wrong, I'm not standing up for mean kids, troublemakers, or haters. They *do* need to learn that constant torment and treating others poorly is unacceptable. They *do* need to understand how their actions can affect the lives of others. But, I am also suggesting that there are two sides to every story. As a professional educator, I've been trained to see and analyze all sides of a situation and find the best solution within the given rules and laws to ensure a safe and effective environment for everyone in terms of social emotional and educational growth.

I'm not saying reporting a situation is always bad, either. Please don't misunderstand my message. However, the approach needs to be one of seeking guidance in how to deal with the situation. "How should I handle this?" as opposed to, "There he is, go get him!" Throughout my teaching career, there have been several times where students have approached me looking for justice against another student who was mean. It usually unfolded this way.

Child 1: He called me a ____.

Child 2: Because he said ____.

Child 1: Well, that was because he ____.

The first time this happened, it didn't take long to realize I was getting into a trap! If I sided with Child 1, then I would be looked at as favoring that one. Child 2 will then dislike Child 1 even more and lose trust in me. If I would have sided with Child 2, then Child 1 would lose trust in me and hate Child 2 even more. Either way, someone's feelings would be hurt, the hatred between them would grow and the torment and retaliation would continue. Parents, if you have more than one child, you know exactly how this game works.

### *There's Got To Be Another Way*

On the other side of the coin lies another approach. An approach that understands the human brain and the development of children throughout their entire lives: a psychological approach. You see, a mental health professional realizes that no matter how hard you try, you cannot change the world around someone. They understand that each person is able to control their own thoughts, emotions and reactions; they just may need a little guidance, help and training to do it. So, a counselor, or psychologist, will coach the target to handle their situations on their own.

A mental health professional understands that, since bullying is an imbalance of power, the best, and easiest, answer is to balance the power. Tip the scales back to even. Empower the target. Once they see they *can* handle the situation on their own, and that they have the tools, tips and skills to do so, the child will grow in resilience, self-confidence and self-esteem, and be able to continue on that positive track for the rest of their lives. Laws cannot do that. Internationally renown school psychologist Izzy Kalman stated that, "In fact, when we lobby for anti-bullying laws, we are declaring the failure of psychology."[14]

Mental health professionals know that you can't strengthen the weak by weakening the strong. And rather than solve all the target's problems for them, teachers, parents and those in the mental health field should teach, mentor and coach students how to deal with the problems themselves. I think, sometimes, our well-intended, good-hearted efforts to help protect our kids can often have the opposite effect. Psychologist Dr. Susan Eva Porter also asserts that "the commonly accepted definition of bullying promotes victimhood, not resilience, and that is terribly problematic considering that resilience is an essential ingredient for success in life."[15]

Everyone understands the fact that kids won't learn math if adults do the homework for them. At least teachers *hope* that's a well-understood fact. It's fine for a parent, helper or tutor to be there providing guidance and help through the math problems. But, obviously, the goal is for the student to be able to do the work by themselves. It's the same thing with dealing with social problems. The only way students learn self-esteem and self-confidence is by going through situations and, with help and guidance along the way, putting specific strategies into practice and getting past obstacles themselves. If the goals are self-esteem and self-confidence to overcome their daily social problems, realize the common denominator of those goals is *self*.

---

[14] Izzy Kalman, "The 'Anti-Bully Law' Oxymoron", Psychology Today, December 20, 2009

[15] Porter, *Bully Nation,* 45

In little league or kids sports, there are players and there are coaches, obviously. Coaches know how to the win the game. If the players listen and follow the coach's instructions, they stand a better chance at winning. However, how crazy would it be if the coach went out onto the field or court and played the game *for* the players? For one, they can't. And secondly, the kids wouldn't learn anything. That's why the coaches have practice and then, when it comes to game time, they stay on the sidelines and hope the players remember to execute properly. Regardless, they are there to coach, not do it *for* the kids.

One last analogy: It's similar to the old adage, "Give a man a fish and he eats for a day. Teach him to fish and he eats for a lifetime." If you fight your child's battles for them, sure they may escape some ill feelings for that day. But, if you can teach your child to handle their social problems on their own, as a mentor, you will get the joy of watching them grow into an epitome of self-confidence, self-esteem and self-advocacy.

We're all on the same page. We want the best for our kids. Emotionally, physically, and educationally. Once we all get on the same page and realize that true resilience is not built by being protected from adversity and struggles, and that you need adversity to build resilience, everyone wins. We don't want kids to be phased by insults and mean words. We don't want kids to be phased by a push or a shove here and there. Otherwise, how can they ever survive sports or public transportation?

Anti-bully laws are incredibly difficult to enforce. If a bullying case makes it to a higher committee or court, it is nearly impossible to prove. Why? Because in court, they look at the definition of bullying, and then things fall apart.

1) Imbalance of power: Since the power imbalance in bullying is mainly psychological and emotional, it's very difficult to prove such an imbalance between two kids.

2) Intent to cause harm: Intent is difficult to prove. What one person calls "an intentional act of emotional or psychological dominance," another may call a joke. Parents, have you ever scolded a child for doing something only to have them answer, "I didn't mean

it. It was an accident. I was just kidding." Or, anything like that? The same defense is often used in regards to bullying laws. The burden then falls on the prosecution to prove them wrong, which is nearly impossible. You can't get into the aggressor's head, scan their thoughts and pull out the one that said, "Yup, I made that kid feel like a loser on purpose."

3) Repeated over time: How many times must the behavior be repeated? 3 times? 5 times? 10 times? Maybe it's over a span of 6 months? But, what if, during that 6 month period, the aggressor was actually civil and the students actually got along?

All of these aspects of anti-bullying laws are not concrete. They're actually quite subjective. Just like any other case, if any single one of the three points is not able to be proven without a shadow of a doubt, the entire case is negated and will be thrown out. This is the main reason why bullying cases are rarely prosecuted, and if they are, never amount to anything.

# INSIDER SECRETS

I was still teaching when I got into this industry. As I was researching and learning all of this content (and unlearning everything I thought I knew), I went through my district's anti-bullying policies with a fine-toothed comb. Not surprising, it was just like everything else.

As time went on, word about my stance, methods and passion got around. Teachers, kids and parents began to make some noise and catch on to the fact that, "Hmm...maybe Mr. Scheufele has a point here." Well, word got back to human resources and the district head of student services and I was given an immediate reprimand with a warning. Essentially, if I didn't quiet down and "stop pointing out the flaws in the district's anti-bullying policy while promoting my own ideas and interests," I'd be let go. I was essentially told to be a teacher that came to work every day, do what I was paid to do and go home. I was allowed to take my personal days to go and perform speaking engagements, but I could not mention anything about my methods or teachings anywhere in the district. Needless to say, at the end of the school year I resigned and jumped into this line of work full-time.

Scary? Sure. The right decision? Absolutely. So, with that, I am about to reveal some insider secrets. What are schools doing? What aren't they doing? What is working? What isn't working? Why? Fasten your seatbelt.

Almost all policies state that the district will provide training to teachers, staff and volunteers. (Some even say "comprehensive training.") What is included in such trainings? They last roughly 45 minutes, if they start on time.[16] Many times, there is one training session per year performed by one of the school's guidance counselors whose only knowledge of bullying is the district's anti-bullying policy. (Even if they do have more knowledge, they are told to stay within the lines.) I've even sat through a few trainings where the counselor read the policy word for word from a bland PowerPoint presentation.

All the while, the teachers and staff sit in these meetings and trainings seemingly numb to the information because it is just another "sit-n-git" style session, boring them out of their minds. It's not that they don't care about bullying. Trust me, they do. They don't want to see your kid, or anyone else's, hurt. But, they are not getting any valuable information. No meat. No substance. No valuable takeaways. Every time I have asked a teacher what they learned from any bullying training, do you know what they told me? "NOTHING!" The same old information is regurgitated every single time. After they leave the meetings, there's usually one of two things that happen. One, they go back to their rooms and get on with their day, forgetting about what they just heard. Two, they discuss how ridiculous the meeting just was because, "if they're going to just read from a PowerPoint, why not just send us the PowerPoint in an email and let us read it?" On top of that, they are also discussing how the same old "solutions" aren't working.

I have interviewed a great deal of teachers from schools all around the country. I've asked them all the same question: "If a student came to you for help with bullying, what does your training tell you to do?" The answers are overwhelmingly disturbing. The most common answer I get is, "I don't really know."

They don't know? Come on! They've sat through so many trainings. How can they not know?

Another answer I hear is, "It doesn't matter. We tell the kids to talk to an assistant principal, principal or counselor, but nothing is

---

[16] Faculty meetings rarely ever start on time.

ever done. They get some information, talk to the alleged bully who denies everything, and send both kids back to class."

Wait a second. I thought there was comprehensive training on how to handle things. This is where the anti-bullying policies have fallen short and failed us. All bark and no bite. Empty promises. Why isn't anything changed? Simple. Nobody is willing to speak up, tell their superiors that they are wrong and things need to be done differently.

## *Student Programs*

Almost every policy states that school districts will provide students with strategies aimed at stopping and/or preventing bullying. This is often done in many ways; usually through guidance counselor lessons and school assemblies.

The guidance counselor lessons, you guessed it, often mirror the teacher trainings. The kids, just like the teachers, rarely get anything out of seeing the same face and same voice reading from the same PowerPoint. One student told me that the only way she can bear those lessons is to imagine the counselor as Charlie Brown's teacher. {Wah wah wah wah wah...}[17]

School assemblies *can* be effective. After all, sometimes familiarity can breed contempt, so schools will often bring in an outside program or speaker to supplement the classroom lessons. However, most of them are far from helpful. How do I know? Again, I ask questions. I listen. I've sat through many assemblies and studied the message. While many assemblies provide great entertainment, the needed content and effective messaging are often sacrificed for the sake of that entertainment. Here's an example.

While I was teaching in a middle school, a local anti-bullying program was invited to present their assembly to the students. They were a band. In fact, they were a very good band. They had lights, fog, video screens, live instruments, and played a variety of popular songs the kids knew and loved.

---

[17] I'm not going to lie, I was happily surprised that she had seen Charlie Brown.

After 20 minutes of music, one of the singers grabbed the microphone and told her story of how she was bullied when she was in school. After her story, she read a definition of bullying from her iPad. Yeah, you read that right. The *leader* of the anti-bullying assembly **read** the definition of bullying from an iPad. She then told students the same old strategies: ignore it, walk away and tell an adult. After that, 20 more minutes of music and dismissal. The assembly was incredibly entertaining. Like I said, they were a very good band. But, in talking to some of the students afterwards, they felt that they were no more aware of how to handle bullying than when they entered. Here are some actual quotes from students after that assembly:

*"They were good, but I didn't learn anything."*

*"None of the things they told us to do actually work. If we tell a teacher, the teacher tells us to go talk to a counselor or make a report in the office. But nothing ever happens after that."*

*"If they're going to pull us out of class, at least teach us something useful."*

I was blown away when I talked to these kids. They realized there was no substance to the message and, even though the program was entertaining, it offered no real significance. There were no takeaways. No call to action. Nothing that students could remember in their tough situations to help solve the issue. Just a cool concert.

Not all outside programs and assemblies are bad, though.[18] I would just encourage schools to:

1) Dig into the teachings of the program and make sure the philosophies align with what is ultimately best for the students - before they are hired. What are the take-aways? What will the students learn?

2) Don't rule out quality programs based on cost. There's always a way to get the funding. Often, you get what you pay for. (The band was free, by the way.)

---

[18] I'll, of course, advocate for mine. :)

3) While entertainment value is important, content is crucial. Don't go for what's bright and shiny. Go for what will leave a lasting impression and bring results.

## *Rewards?*

It seems that there is a certain trend that is rearing its head in schools recently. It started from a good place, I think, but it has snowballed out of control.

The notion of rewarding students to step forward has been around for years. It began as a program to encourage students to come forward to work with administration and law enforcement to track down and stop criminal behavior. Countless schools around the country have posters in the halls advertising monetary rewards for tips and information leading to the intervention or solving of a crime or infraction of a school policy. They usually advertise anonymity for the tipster and a simple number for the students to call or text their tip to. The hope is that kids will come forward with their knowledge of things like hidden drugs, weapons on campus, looming fights, forthcoming acts of violence or turning in a perpetrator of a past crime. Anonymously! No more "snitches get stitches." No more fear of coming forward! Sounds good, right?

Well, unfortunately, I'm starting to see these posters in schools now for bullying. One poster said, *"Report bullying and you could be paid in as little as 24 hours for your tip."* What has this done? In many cases, it has increased the number of incidents reported, which may seem like a good thing, until we hear the fact that many of the incidents reported are either false, an attempt to cash in on some free money, or minuscule incidents such as making faces or calling someone a name one time.

It has completely taken the definition of "bullying" off the rails. What's worse is that administrators are chasing wind and investigating a huge number of empty-ended situations thereby leaving their true responsibilities untouched and piling up on their desks. On top of that, consider the fact that each incident investigation can cost a school district up to $1,500. Per incident! If you add that to the potential reward money that could be paid, you have quite the hefty cost for the school district. That's your tax dollars at work, by the way. And when you consider how underpaid and underfunded classrooms are, it makes for an angle that nobody thought to consider when it was first implemented.

In 2018, one school district in Colorado actually got into some hot water over the hotline approach. A female high school student ended up being the target of mistreatment and mean behavior because of the district's reporting hotline.

*Wait...what?*

Believe it or not, some students took it upon themselves to falsely report that the girl was suicidal and had been using drugs that were provided by her parents. They made this false report several times. What followed for the student were several instances of being pulled out of class to endure embarrassing interviews and interrogation sessions, all because students were abusing the very thing that was supposed to solve the problem: the hotline.

Shortly after, this target's friends became targets of the exact same behavior. False reports by students who wanted to make their lives miserable. The "bullies" were abusing the solution system and creating more problems! [19]

As if that wasn't enough, that left the lawmakers in Colorado scrambling to fix things. One lawmaker said that there needs to be a system to better track false reports along with more education implemented to teach students that making false reports is actually a crime. But, there's a problem with that. The founder of the hotline company said that tracking the reports is very difficult because what one school may report as "false," another school may report the same incident as "unsubstantiated." The reporting is subjective. Around and around and around...

Rather than spending so much valuable time and money to fix a broken, flawed and easily-manipulated system, how about ditching the system and focusing on solutions that empower students to be resilient, and equip them with the social skills they need to deal with the ills of their social lives?

_____

[19] I didn't need a crystal ball to see that coming. Yet, many were surprised.

## No Bully Zones!

Forgive me if I sound like a smart aleck, but I really want to illustrate the futility of this. Fellow bullying expert and great friend Jeff Veley[20] recently told me a great story.

Jeff arrived at a school in which he was supposed to speak to students and staff regarding bullying prevention. While walking down the hall with the principal, Jeff noticed a poster on the wall that said "This is a NO BULLY ZONE!" Jeff, being the hilarious guy he is, stopped under the poster and refused to move. The principal was baffled. He said, "Jeff, the gym is this way. Why did you stop?"

Jeff answered, "Well if this is the 'no bully zone,' I don't want to leave it and risk getting bullied."

The principal froze, dropped his jaw and realized the blunder caused by the poster.

Why don't "no bully zones" work? Well…how big is the zone? Just around the poster? Does it extend 5 feet? 10 feet? What if a student doesn't want to get bullied? Should they stay next to the poster and not go to class? Wouldn't that make an already embarrassed target stand out even more? Do we need a poster for every classroom, bathroom, office, etc? And my favorite: Do we really expect a mean kid to see the poster and say, "Oh wait, this is a 'no bully zone.' I should stop." The answer is "No." I know I'm being a little tongue-in-cheek. I understand what the poster means, but let's be honest. If one student wants to be mean to another, they are going to be mean. They don't care about a poster, sign or an invisible zone. The only thing they care about is if an adult is around or not.

## Fine!

Some school districts are participating in another solution to combat bullying: fining the parents of the alleged bully. Some states require that the parents of the alleged "bully" pay fines in excess of

---

[20] Jeff also has quite the refined pallet when it comes to tacos.

$1000 per incident. I have to admit, when I first heard of this, I was on board.

I am a HUGE proponent of parental responsibility. If you raise your children right at home behind closed doors, they will be more likely to act properly in school. If you don't take the time and care to teach your children right from wrong, and they act up, you, as the parent, are partly, if not mostly, to blame.[21] So, it made sense to me, that if the kid acts up in school, the parents should be held somewhat responsible and take some of the responsibility for their child's behavior. At first, fines really sounded like a great idea.

But then, I started to think about what could go wrong. And then it hit me. Could you imagine, as a parent, receiving the following phone call from your child's school?

Parent: *Hello?*

School: *Hello, this is Mrs. Smith from Pine Lane Middle School.*

Parent: *Uh huh…*

School: *We just wanted to inform you that you are being fined $1000.*

Parent: *WHAT?! Why?!*

School: *Because your child is a bully and has been bullying other students.*

You can imagine the linguistic sparks that would fly after that.

Even worse, let's say you don't even receive a phone call. Let's say that the school sends you a bill in the mail. Or, tells your child to tell you. Or, sends a note home with your child. Or, maybe they call you in for a conference and tell you once you are seated in the school conference room. Either way, it's not going to be a pretty conversation.

---

[21] That may sound harsh, but it's my opinion. You can have your own and disagree with me if you wish.

So what's wrong with the "fine" approach?

The punishment is separate from the offense. The thinking that fining the parents will have a positive, long-lasting effect on the child is flawed. The expectation is that the behavior will be changed immediately, completely ignoring any and all parts of childhood behavioral development. Creating new and different punishments for the mean kids does not help the targets. It doesn't empower anyone.

The goal *should* be for parents and schools to work together to make the schools a better place. This approach accomplishes the opposite. Not only does it halt the growth of a working relationship between parents and schools, it throws it into reverse and stomps on the gas. Yes, parents need to be parents and teach their children to respect the feelings of others, but instead of thinking of new ways to punish the offenders, how about we put some brain power into how we can empower *all* children in order to prevent the issue from getting blown up to these proportions in the first place?

### *The Illusion*

One of the questions I get asked the most as I work with parents is, "Why does it seem like schools aren't doing anything?" In fact, some people don't even ask. They make sure the world knows that their child's school is "lazy, ignorant and careless in regards to their actions against bullying."

It's a completely valid question. Schools know that these behaviors are taking place within their walls, so why on Earth don't they do something about it? Are they really that naïve to believe that it isn't happening? Are they just ignoring it and hoping it will go away? Do they do just enough to make it look like they're trying to combat it so they could survive a lawsuit?[22] Do they just not care?

The easy answers to those questions are:

- *Are they really that naïve to believe that it isn't happening?* No, of course not.

---

[22] I like to call this the "smoke and mirrors" approach.

- *Are they just ignoring it and hoping it will go away?* In a lot of cases, yes. In one school, a group of parents was up in arms about the amount of bullying behavior that was occurring, so they took their concerns to the principal. Shockingly, the principal completely disregarded their claims and actually said, "There's no bullying on this campus. We don't have a bullying problem."

- *Do they do just enough to make it look like they're trying to combat it so they could survive a lawsuit?* Again, in many cases, yes. School districts have highly paid attorneys on retainer to write their policies and ensure that they stay out of court. And, because of all of the other things on their plates (academic standards and such), you can bet that many schools are doing just enough to keep themselves out of a sticky, costly situation.

I interviewed one assistant principal that told me some troubling information.

**Warning: You may want to sit down for this one. Grab a pillow. Step away from any sharp objects. Maybe get a beverage to help calm yourself...a strong one.**

This assistant principal divulged that many schools are required to keep record of their disciplinary actions for students. That includes in-school suspensions, out-of-school suspensions, expulsions, temporary alternative school placements, etc. Usually, anything greater than a detention. And, at specified times throughout the school year, those records must be submitted to either the district, state or governing body. Sounds ok so far, right?

Well, once those reports are submitted, the schools will get a grade, or rating, based on their disciplinary numbers. This grade, in many cases, becomes public knowledge and will then determine things like future enrollment, resources, funding and even job security, or lack thereof. (You see where I'm going with this, don't you?)

So, what are some schools doing? Any combination of these three things:

1. They are falsely reporting their discipline numbers. Cooking the books. Turning in falsified data to preserve the reputation of the school.

2. They are not providing the discipline that is specified in their handbooks and policies. For example, let's say that a school's policy says that if a student is found guilty of "bullying" another student, he will receive 2 days of in-school suspension upon the first offense, 5 days of in-school suspension for the second offense, and out-of-school suspension for any subsequent offenses. Unfortunately, in order to avoid a negative discipline record, the administrator will catch the offender in the hallway or call him to the office, give him a quick, stern "talking to" and send him back to class. A slap on the wrist, basically. Nothing that needs reporting.

3. The school chooses not to act at all because it is buried under so many layers of other policies and guidelines that the actual investigation and punishment of the offender borders on the infringement of the offender's rights.

It's maddening to think that any one of those situations are true. But, guess what! They are. Truth be told, it could be a combination of those. I've seen it all. However, from my experience, I think there's a bigger reason at play.

I'm willing to give schools and administrators the benefit of the doubt. The vast majority of them actually **DO** care about your kids. The vast majority **DO** want the best for your kids – more than just good standardized test scores. Behind closed doors, the vast majority of them are not into "smoke and mirrors" to just save their hides. The vast majority of schools **ARE** actively trying to make campuses better, safer and more secure. And, I think I can confidently say that no principal wants to end up on the evening news because of a viral video, suicide or mass shooting that stemmed from the big, bad "B" word.

Schools have all of these policies in place. They have the posters. They have the PowerPoint lessons. They show the videos. They have assemblies. They have banners on their websites that boast of their intolerance for bullying. They even provide the website links to the district's anti-bullying policies and anonymous reporting forms. But, kids are still being hurt, tormented, ridiculed and emotionally harmed daily. Why?

In my humble, honest (and accurate) opinion, I believe that, despite their good-natured, well-intentioned efforts, all of these policies stem from flawed logic and misinformation. They come from the following positions:

- Continue to change the definition of "bullying" to include any possible behavior that could possibly hurt someone's feelings
- Make every student stop being mean.
- Everybody be nice to each other 100% of the time.
- Emphasize the punishments for being a "bully" to deter the behavior

The problem is that schools blindly follow the policies that they are handed and continue to get frustrated with the lack luster results of their efforts. The reason? The authors of the policies are ignoring simple psychology and buying into the myth that rules can make a 100% utopian environment.[23]

---

[23] Chances are these authors are also several years removed from the classroom environment, sit in an air conditioned office with an expensive desk and leather chair, and have almost no connection with any students in their district.

# IT'S JUST NOT WORKING OUT

We all want the best for our kids. As a father, I know I do. We hate to see them suffer and go through hard times. So, we offer advice. It usually comes from the heart - as it should. When dealing with another mean kid, we tell our children things like: ignore it, walk away, tell an adult and fight back. The majority of schools are teaching the same things; blindly, I might add. (Maybe not "fight back" though.) I love to ask students how those approaches work - knowing their answers before they speak, of course. The answers are always the same. The approaches actually fail more than they work. In fact, they may be making things worse. What's more, many students *know* they don't work and have become numb, and even contemptuous, towards these pieces of advice.

## *Ignore It*

One of the first go-to remedies for dealing with aggressors, and mean people in general, is to ignore them. Pretend they don't exist. By doing so, they will see that their behavior has no affect and will ultimately stop. However, as we'll see, that's not the best way to handle things.

I'm probably dating myself here, but I'm going to relate this to an old favorite video game. That's right friends, I'm going old school Nintendo. Super Mario Brothers 3. In the game, there were some levels where Mario encountered ghosts. You couldn't kill the ghosts - it was impossible. If Mario so much as touched them, he died. But, there was one thing that made the ghosts interesting. If Mario turned his back on them, they came after him with scary looks and fangs, ultimately leading to Mario's demise. If Mario turned and looked toward them, however, they covered their faces and froze right where they were. It's almost like they knew Mario's bravery and only had the guts to come and get him when his back was turned.

Ignoring aggressors and mean people follows the same logic. Ignoring them doesn't make them go away. They know that game. They are like the ghosts in Super Mario 3. Once you try to ignore them, they're going to keep coming. They are going to keep doing and saying things because they know it's working. Ultimately, you can't solve a problem by ignoring it.

Think of it this way. Let's say that you're driving down the road and your "check engine" light comes on. I know, it's one of the most annoying things in the world. But, what do so many people do? They think, "I'm sure it's nothing. I mean, my car is running fine. I don't hear any noises. It doesn't feel any different. It's probably nothing." Ignore. Ignore. Ignore. Two weeks later, you find yourself on the side of the highway calling for a tow because something decided to quit working. Then, the mechanic tells you that if you had only brought it in when the light first came on, the repair would only be $300 instead of the current $1500.

Ignoring anything doesn't make it go away. Car problems, health issues, persistent mean behavior. There's no solution. No resolution. No empowerment. I can't tell you how many students have told me that ignoring mean behavior doesn't work. Every time I ask a student why, they say something like, "It doesn't solve the problem. They just keep doing it. They know you'll break eventually."

Simply put, **you can't solve a problem by ignoring it.**

### *Walk Away*

Another common remedy is to walk away. Just turn around and walk away. This one falls along some of the same lines as ignoring. The thinking is that by removing yourself from the situation and getting away from the mean behavior, it will stop.

Traveling the country and working with students of all ages, I've asked how using the "walk away" strategy works. Here's how one of those interviews went with a panel of middle school students.

Me: *What about walking away?*

Students: {Eye rolls and loud exhales}

Me: *Ok. What makes you react that way?*

Student 1: *It makes you look weak.*

Me: *In whose eyes?*

Student 1: *Everyone. The bully, your friends, people watching.*

Student 2: *Yeah, it almost looks like you're running away from your problems.*

Student 3: *Yeah, and they, like, just follow you and keep on doing it anyway. It's like it turns into, like, a game of Tag, or Chase or whatever.*

Me: *Ooo, why is that?*

Student 3: *Because they know you're getting mad.*

Me: *And they like that?*

Students: *Yes.*

Me: *Why?*

Student 3: *I don't know. I guess it's fun for them.*

Student 1: *Yeah, it's like they have fun making you mad so they want to keep doing it even if you are walking away.*

Let me add something here. If there is any immediate danger of objective harm (damage to body or property), then yes, get out of the situation right away. But, generally speaking, walking away often turns into a game of Cat and Mouse where the aggressor gets an added bonus of a chase with their tormenting. No solution. No resolution. No empowerment.

And, as many students have told me, **you can't solve a problem by walking away from it.**

### *Tell an Adult/Report It*

A very typical remedy to mean behavior is to tell an adult. Tell a teacher, counselor, coach, assistant principal, principal… someone! Why? Because the hope is that the adult will go and tell the mean kid to quit being mean, the mean kid will obey the rule of authority and the conflict will dissolve and everything will be great again.

Are you laughing, too? Students usually laugh at the absurdity of that notion when I bring it up. But, why? That's how it works in the movies and on TV right?

Don't you remember the old 1950's black and white TV shows like *Leave it to Beaver* and *Dennis the Menace*?[24] Those shows did a great job of instilling values in 30 minutes. And, oh, how easy it was to solve a conflict! The mean kid did something to the target. The target told an adult. The adult sat both kids down and made the mean kid apologize. "Gee, I'm sorry Wally. I'll never be mean to you again." Then they went out to play baseball and everything was hunky dory again. Maybe that worked in the 1950's, but things are a bit different now. Telling, tattling or informing on your peers is one of the most detestable things a kid can do in the eyes of their peers.[25]

I recently spoke with a mom, Jen, whose son was in this situation. Apparently, her son, Holden, had endured some unkind treatment from a teammate. So, Holden went to Mama Bear. Jen went to the parents of the troublemaker and requested that they make their son "stop his bullying behavior." What followed was, in my mind, predictable, yet awful. The troublemaker, the majority of

---

[24] I caught reruns on Nick at Nite as a kid.

[25] Again, as I said earlier, if there is immediate danger to someone's body or property, go tell. When safety and security is an issue, go get an adult right away.

the team and several other friends began to exclude Holden at lunch and from social activities. Jen realized that both she and Holden had broken "the code." She confided that, rather than fight the battle for him, she should have just equipped and coached Holden with how to handle the situation on his own.

Side note: I instructed Jen to have the boys sit down and calmly discuss things using specific conflict resolution language. Each apologized for the effects of their own behaviors and transgressions. The boys made up and have agreed to disagree, but to work together for the good of the team.

Even just thinking back to my own grade school career, there was a policy called **Snitches Get Stitches.** It didn't take a rocket scientist to know what that meant. If you told on someone, no matter the reason, they found you, and you got hurt. That thinking still lives on in schools today all over the country. I've seen it first hand.

Even students know that telling an adult or reporting mean behavior hardly ever works. Many students have told me, in no uncertain terms, that they have little to no faith in the authority of teachers, counselors and administrators to help solve their problems. There's very little trust. Students think it's all but pointless to try to get an adult to try to solve their problems for them. (More on that point in a second.)

What typically happens when a student tells? One of two things.

1) Nothing. The adult is either too busy to track down all facets of a student's social problem, or the students involved are not forthcoming with the truth, leading the adult down a dead end path.

2) Things are made worse. When an adult intervenes, accuses one party of being a "bully" and reprimands them, whether deserved or not, the animosity between both students skyrockets and the situation is often made worse.

Now, this is where I usually have to calm people down. I am not saying, "Don't go to an adult for help." Please don't misunderstand my message. One of the ways kids learn to deal with their social emotional problems is by seeking the help of an adult. Resilience is a learned trait. However, a psychologically and sociologically healthy approach to seeking the help of an adult begins with this question: "How can I solve this problem?"

Did you catch that? How can *I* solve it? Not, "There he is! Go get him! Make him stop! Do it for me!" There's a difference. One helps to build resilience, the other doesn't. One is in the spirit of getting someone in trouble, while the other seeks helpful tips to build resilience and solve problems on one's own.

Throughout my teaching career, almost every time a student came to me with a social emotional problem, such as bullying, they asked, "Mr. Scheufele, how can I solve this? How can I make them stop? What can I do? How can I...I...I...?"[26] Kids *want* to be able to do things on their own. They *want* to learn. But, like anything else, they have to be *taught*.

When a child tells or tattles without seeking the knowledge of how to solve their social problems on their own, and expects others to solve their social problems for them, any of these three things can happen:

First, it creates a learned helplessness, which is also a common symptom of depression. Children with learned helplessness develop an expectation that future situations will be out of their control leaving them no choice but to rely on others to solve their problems, reject the help to change and abandon nearly all hope.

Second, it creates a victim mentality. We all know people who play the victim card. They can't take responsibility for themselves, nothing is their fault, nothing is fair, they seem to have no backbone and they end up being overly reliant on others to help them get through life.

---

[26] Have you picked up on the key word there?

Third, children who fall into this category often use the authority of adults to hold an abusive power over their enemies and exercise it at will. I have known several students over the years who would either fabricate or exaggerate stories about their enemies in order to keep the teacher on their side and keep their enemies in a negative light.[27]

**Help children understand the difference between telling/tattling and actually seeking the knowledge to solve their social problems on their own.**

### *Fight Back*

I'm willing to bet that almost everyone was told the same type of story by their grandfather. My grandfather was no different. Whenever I would tell him about a kid at school that was giving me trouble, he would break out *his* story. It went something like this...

When he was in the army in WWII as a military police officer, Pop (that's what I called him) was faced with a lieutenant that didn't see eye to eye with him. But, since the lieutenant was a higher rank, there wasn't much Pop could do. They exchanged unpleasant words on occasion and grew to understand that they did not care for each other. They couldn't stand each other. One day things came to a head, and Pop stood up to the lieutenant and said, "Meet me in the latrine and we'll settle this."[28]

Once at the latrine, the dukes (fists) went up and it became a backyard boxing match...for about 10 seconds. According to Pop, the lieutenant took a swing and missed. Pop countered with a right cross and "knocked 'em on his...." You get the picture.

Pop loved to tell that story. But it was his way of telling me to stand up for myself and not to let anyone, no matter how big or

---

[27] If you have more than one child at home, this is also another way that sibling rivalry shows its face.

[28] The latrine was essentially a community hole or ditch where the soldiers went to the bathroom.

old, push me around. There was just one problem. The rules in the latrine are a bit different than the rules in school.

It made for a great, heroic story. And on the wings of such tales, several people, adults and kids included, encouraged me to fight back. They would say, "Next time they make fun of you, just swing and hit one as hard as you can. Then they'll see that you're tougher than you look. They'll see you're a force to be reckoned with. They'll have to respect you. Even if you lose the fight, they'll at least know you're not going to take any more of their stuff." At this, student audiences usually cheer and clap because they've heard similar things in their lives. Fight back. Show 'em how tough you are.

Unfortunately, that's not always the best option. Generally, the situation usually goes something like this: Little Johnny gets picked on and teased by big, mean Butch every single day. But, Butch never gets in trouble because the teacher never sees it, or if she does, she just treats the situation as talking out of turn and nothing really happens. However, one day, little Johnny reaches his tipping point and slugs Butch in the face and breaks his nose.

Most people would then say, "Go Johnny! Way to stand up for yourself! You really showed him!" And while it may seem that little Johnny has won the day, *he* is the one that gets suspended from school and, possibly, slapped with an assault charge from Butch's parents. Why? Because Johnny started the fight. Yes, he was just standing up for himself against a mean kid, but that fact doesn't matter to the powers that be. It may have worked in the past. You know, the old "Meet me behind the playground at 3:00" approach. The downside is that, now, according to most school policies, it doesn't matter when the altercation happened or whether the altercation occurred on or off school property. If the incident has anything to do with school, anything at all, it is a school problem. So, because of the rules and laws that are in place, fighting back is not the best decision. Besides, if the goal is to reduce and resolve conflicts in schools, why escalate it by introducing or participating in physical violence?

## *Stand By Me*

Simply put, a bystander is anyone who is present for an event or incident but does not participate. A witness, if you will. Over the last few years, there is a big push for bystanders of bullying incidents to be more than just onlookers. The push is for them to get involved, speak up and be an UP-stander. The thinking is that when bystanders become up-standers, the aggressor will stop and the conflict will be over.

Yes, there are studies that do show that when a person intervenes in a conflict, the conflict has a greater chance of dissolving. Many situations like fights and crimes are thwarted because someone steps in. Bullying and social aggression can be very similar. What are the pros of being an up-stander? You are viewed as a good samaritan. You helped someone out. You may have stopped a situation from going from bad to worse. You possibly saved someone from mental and emotional torment. You're a hero.

I know you're probably thinking, "Chris, this all sounds so wonderful! There can't possibly be any cons." Hold my Dr. Pepper.[29]

A very popular fast food chain put out a commercial in 2017. I won't mention the name of the chain, but if you picture a burger and a male ruler of a country who wears a crown, you can figure it out. The commercial featured a group of young teenage actors in the restaurant. One kid portrayed the target and the other three kids portrayed "bullies." Hidden cameras were placed around the restaurant to see what real customers/bystanders would do if they witnessed "bullying" behavior. Would they intervene and save the target? Or, would they just sit back, give an awkward glance and pretend nothing was happening? The goal was to find out how many real customers would be up-standers.

Much to the surprise of many, only about 12% of the bystanders did anything. The other 88% glanced over and did nothing, leaving us, the viewers, to shake our heads in dismay and think less of those people, wondering if their parents hadn't taught

---

[29] I know the saying is, "Hold my beer," but I don't drink. So, Dr. Pepper it is!

them any better. But, let's look at some facts. While the commercial was not a legitimate social science experiment, it definitely reflected the truth about up-stander numbers. Why so few? I'm glad you asked.

First and foremost, being an effective up-stander takes a certain social savvy that most people do not possess. More often than not, many people don't want to meddle in others' business, especially if they don't know all of the details of the situation. Moreover, an ideal up-stander has the ability to navigate complicated social situations and discern what they are dealing with very quickly, in an impartial, unbiased way. For example, they have the ability to listen *through* foul language instead of allowing it to flare up their own emotions. Is that easy for a tween or teen? No. At least, not the majority. Students are constantly in a stage of social emotional development, no matter what age, and it is very difficult for them to be able to navigate their own problems, let alone someone else's, in a manner to be able to effectively intervene in a successful way.

Many students have told me that they simply don't know how to be an effective up-stander. They say that the school preaches the practice, but does not give any tips or training on *how* to do it. The lesson just said, "Be an up-stander, not a bystander," and that was it. But, interestingly enough, that tip was followed up with this quote that we've all heard before: "If you stand by and do nothing, you are just as guilty as the bully."

So, let me get this straight. Tell the kids what to do, but not how to do it. Then shame them for not doing it because they weren't taught how. Make them feel guilty for not yet having the skillset, courage or wisdom to read a situation and properly intervene. Sound ridiculous? When I first put that together, I just about hit the ceiling in anger and disbelief. Moving on…

Looking at it from another angle, telling bystanders to intervene has the potential to put them into the role of a judge - having to discern who is right or wrong in a situation. This usually leads to taking sides, alienating one of the parties and assigning judgmental labels without knowing all sides of the story. It essentially turns kids into police and investigators; and that is not their job.

Up-standers can also unintentionally redirect attention towards themselves. This can be good, in a sense that it takes the attention away from the target, allowing the target to get away. However, it can also be bad. An old Jewish proverb says, "Meddling in the quarrels of others is like grabbing a stray dog by the ears." What does that mean? Simple. If you grab a stray dog by the ears, you will get bit. I have seen many situations and read several stories where students have gotten hurt or even killed by intervening in a situation that was not their business, just trying to stick up for someone else. While these cases may be rare, they still happen, and they are a real danger to our kids.

Lastly, it doesn't empower the target. In some cases, a target can create a learned helplessness by always expecting someone else to jump in and rescue them. I like to pose this question: Is it easier to teach 1,000 people to be the kind of social savvy, effective up-standers we need, or to teach one student to be resilient and empower them with the tools to solve their own social emotional problems?

Now, remember, I'm talking about social aggression here. Of course, if there is any impending danger to someone's body or property, yes, yank them out of there! If there is any hint of sexual misconduct, get in and get them out! If someone's rights are being infringed upon, get them out. If someone can't seem to get away from a tormentor, help them get away. But, when it comes to social aggression, teasing, or name-calling, I have yet to find an effective "up-stander" program that is able to be implemented by 100% of a student body. In my opinion, the best kind of up-stander is a person of great resilience who can pass on the skills and techniques of solving social squabbles to their peers in efforts to empower them for the future.

### I'm Leaving on a Jet Plane

I've met several people, students and parents, that tell me they moved - relocated their entire family and lives - for the sole purpose of escaping a problem at school. Of course, this saddens me greatly. I especially hated to see this as a teacher, because the majority of kids that fell into this category were some of my favorites.[30] It's completely infuriating that a child can be tormented to the point where the family feels that they have no other choice than to uproot everything and get out of Dodge.

I'm a dad. I love my kids. I completely understand the desire and need to protect my kids from things that could potentially have a traumatic, negative impact on their lives. I get it. If your child is in physical danger, yes, get them out of there. If things have gotten to the point of self harm or suicidal thoughts and feelings, get them help ASAP. But, as a parent, I want you to give an honest look at your child's situation and ask yourself these questions. Are they in any type of legitimate physical danger? Have you exhausted all possible options to help your child cope and thrive in their current environment - up to and including counseling? If you answered no to those, maybe packing up your life isn't quite the answer yet.

Here's some truth, as I've seen this happen time and time again. A change of scenery is no guarantee that your child will be problem free. Every school in every town has at least one kid whose whole goal is to make someone else feel miserable. It doesn't matter what school your child goes to. It doesn't matter what town.

You also have to be careful of the unintended lessons that are being taught. There is a good chance that your child will begin to think that any time they have a problem, you will swoop in and get them out. Or, maybe they'll think that they can run away from every adversity. Friends, let's not take that chance. At the risk of sounding like a broken record, I'm not talking about situations where there is a legitimate threat to their physical wellbeing. By all means, if that is the case, please get them out of there. But, if the issue falls within the spectrum of social aggression - name calling, teasing, rumors, pushing and shoving that does not cause pain, etc. - the best thing to do is to build up their emotional resilience and teach them how to respond to those situations in order to squash any social squabble they face.

---

[30] I mean...umm...teachers don't have favorites.

# THE TRUTH SETS YOU FREE

If you haven't figured it out by now, I'm very pro-truth. Even though the truth may hurt at the time of hearing it, embracing the truth is the only way to begin the healing process. Hearing the truth is like confirming a medical diagnosis. We all either have been diagnosed, or know someone who has been diagnosed, with a serious medical issue. At the time, it stinks. Worry sets in. Doubt clouds our thinking. Questions fly everywhere. What's next?

After the doctor confirms a diagnosis, what does he immediately begin to talk about? Treatment! How can we attack this problem and make things right? What things can be done at home and on your own? What medications can be given? What type of procedures can be performed?

But, what happens if you never go to the doctor? What happens if you ignore the issue? Or worse, what happens if the doctor is wrong about the diagnosis and treats the wrong thing? Things get worse! Regardless, you can't begin to move towards a cure until the truth is discovered. The whole truth and nothing but the truth.

We can't begin to properly help our children solve their "bullying" problems until they understand the truth. In my experience, one of the biggest truths being withheld from kids today is this:

**Not everyone is going to like you and not everyone is going to be your friend.**

When I say that to a group of adults, many heads nod and smiles form as if to say, "Finally, someone has said what we've been thinking." Occasionally I will get an offended look because my "speaking the truth in love" will be mistaken for criticizing how someone should parent their child. Believe me, friends. I am not giving parental criticism. I am simply sharing my experiences and what I have found to be true.

Now, when I say that to a group of students, some of them look at me like I'm crazy, as if to say, "I thought you were a motivational speaker. I'm not feeling very motivated. You should be more positive!" So, I pause, center myself, take a deep breath and say, "I'm positive not everyone is going to like you. And I'm positive not everyone is going to be your friend." It gets a laugh, but it's true!

As adults, we know that the world has nice people and mean people. There are people who are going to treat us like friends and there are people who are going to treat us like bitter enemies. That's just the truth. And that's ok. The truth is that we don't need EVERYONE'S approval. You don't need to be EVERYONE'S friend. An important lesson to teach our children is that once you stop living for the approval of others, life gets so much easier. Once you stop worrying what other people say and think about you, they don't have control over you anymore.

I like to help kids frame the issues of their social status with this exercise:[31]

Think of your favorite athlete. Once you have that person in mind, think of your favorite musician. Got it? Good. Now think of your favorite movie star. Done? Last one: picture the leader of your country. The president, Prime Minister, King, Queen...whatever your situation is.

---

[31] I usually have the students close their eyes and visualize, but it wouldn't make sense for you to do that right now because you wouldn't be able to read the instructions.

From there, I explain the point of the exercise. Those people have more haters than many of us can even imagine. The most popular professional athletes have millions of fans – and millions of haters. Take a baseball player for example. I once heard a statistic about baseball players. In one major league at bat, a baseball player will have more negative said to him and about him than almost anyone else will in a lifetime. Think about it. On any given day, there could be anywhere from 30,000 to 60,000 people in a stadium. If the team is playing an away game, chances are, there won't be many of their hometown fans in the crowd.

Let's say, for all intents and purposes, that the time it takes a batter to leave the dugout, get to the plate, strike out, and walk back to the dugout is about 3 minutes. In that 3 minutes, the batter will have thousands of people screaming all kinds of things at him; some of which he'll be able to hear quite clearly. In addition, there are TV and radio broadcasters saying negative things. Not to mention the listeners and viewers all around the country tuning in and yelling their thoughts at the radios and TVs. That's just one at bat. The guy has to go through that 3-5 times per game, nearly 80 away games per year. Even if we take the low numbers, 30,000 people x 3 at bats x 80 away games per year = 7.2 million people hurling negativity at one batter! That's a lot of weight for one person to carry.

Your favorite musicians have millions of people who love their music – and just as many who can't stand it. Movie stars have millions of people who can't wait to see their next film – and just as many who hate everything they've ever done.

Leaders of countries probably have it the worst. In recent years, we have seen the dislike (or flat out hatred) of presidential candidates grow in ways we've never seen before. The mudslinging between candidates, the jokes by TV show hosts and the jabs by the media have become stronger, more frequent and more filthy over the past few years. For all intents and purposes, again, let's figure that close to half the country doesn't like the president and expresses their negative comments. At this point, the total population of the United States is roughly 320 million people. That means that there could be close to 160 million people around the country saying negative or hateful things about the president. That's a lot of haters!

If those people let the weight of all of that hate get to them, they wouldn't even be able to get out of bed. But, they don't let it bother them. They understand that name-calling, rumors, rude humor, prejudice, judgement, etc. is part of being in the public eye. So, how do they handle it? They are resilient. They have thick skin, they let it bounce off and they continue to move forward. They stay true to themselves. They are happy with who they are and how they are. They don't allow who they are to be shaped by the negative opinions of others.

Once I'm able to frame this perspective for students, they are quick to realize that a couple of people calling them names at school isn't the worst thing in the world. Sure, it stinks at the time, but it's not the end of the world.

There will always be mean people. There will always be people who say mean things, call us names, spread rumors, push and shove, exclude us and try to hurt our feelings. Fact. **We can't control other people. We** *can* **control how we take things and how we respond to them.**

PART 2: HELP!  MY KID IS BEING BULLIED!

# KEEP CALM AND PARENT ON

*Train up a child in the way he should go; and when he is old, he will not depart from it. ~Jewish Proverb*

Imagine this for a moment:

You come home from work. You walk in the door, put your things down, take off your shoes and call your child's name.

No answer.

"Typical," you think. "Probably playing a mind-numbing video game or listening to that crud they call 'music'. Gosh, kids these days have no idea what real music is. The Beatles. Now that was real music."

You walk upstairs and down the hall and knock on the door. "Hunny?"

No answer.

You open the door.[32]

---

[32] It *is your* house, right? You pay the bills. You can open whatever door you want, when you want.

You see your child laying on the bed, face down in the pillow, crying. You walk over, sit on the bed and try to find out what's wrong. Your child tells you that they have been the target of relentless teasing, torment and bullying at school.

On the list of moments that no parent wants to experience with their children, this is definitely one of them. Your child is sobbing and broken because at school, a place where they are supposed to be safe, protected and taken care of, they are faced with horrors and torment on a daily basis.

## *So, What Can You Do?*

First thing's first: Stay calm! Don't freak out. If you freak out, your child will freak out, too. Do you remember when your sweet darling was a little tyke? Remember when they would fall face-first after running so fast that their legs moved faster than their brain? What was the first thing they did when they fell? Chances are, before crying, they looked right up at you to see your reaction. If you freaked out, ran over and made a huge deal out of it, they began to sob uncontrollably. If you showed a bit of empathy but remained calm and coached them to get back up and keep going, chances are they brushed the dirt off their knees and went along just fine.

Listen, empathize, and keep a level head. Yes, to your child, the situation is a big deal. Yes, this could appear to be the biggest crisis they've ever faced. Let them tell you all about it. Listen to everything. Don't interrupt. Don't try to give them advice or instruction until after they've calmed down. Your child is in a hurt, anxious state and they're not ready to be taught yet. Just listen and comfort. Don't pull out your phone and give the school or the "bully's" parents an earful of your angry verbiage laced with your favorite four-letter words and insults that would make a marine wince. Don't post about it on social media. Don't call 911. RELAX!

## *Helicopters and Snowplows*

A common, and quite understandable, reaction is for parents to do one of two things: become a helicopter or a snowplow. Let me explain. In recent years, we've seen the rise of helicopter parents. They are the ones that hover over their children, watch their every move to guard them from the slightest bit of trouble and are essentially overprotective. Child psychologists agree that helicopter parents often do things for their children that their children could, and should, do for themselves. This, in turn, allows for hardly any time for the self-discovery, self-growth and independent development that children of all ages need.

One step beyond helicopter parents are snowplow parents. Snowplow parents are exactly as they sound: they get in front of their kids, mow everything over and blow it out of the way. They clear the path and make sure nothing gets in the way, ensuring the smoothest, easiest road possible for their children. Helicopter and snowplow parenting tactics all come from good places. No parent wants to watch their children suffer. But, if you solve all of your children's problems for them, how will they ever learn? How will they survive society on their own when they grow up?[33]

At the risk of sounding redundant, I like to use the example of math homework. As parents, we know that if we do our kids' math homework *for* them, they won't learn anything and they'll likely fail the test, fail the class and become one of those cashiers who freezes up when someone pays with cash and expects correct change back.[34] Besides, I've never met a teacher that allows parents to sit beside their kids on test day and give them the answers. But, if you do the math homework **with** them, side by side, helping them understand why numbers and letters move around the way they do, and practice various real life applications with them, not only will they be prepared for the test, but they will be a math beast who can dish out correct change faster than you can swipe your debit card.

**Quick tangent story:** When I was a kid, my dad was high up the ladder of a large grocery store chain. I remember him bringing home an old cash register and filling it with spare change and dollar bills from around the house, and we would play *Grocery Store*. Of course, the register did the calculations and that's how I learned to count money. But, he eventually made me figure out the change before punching anything into the register. I had no idea

---

[33] Hint: It won't be because of their looks.

[34] That's a really fun game to play, by the way.

what he was doing at the time. I was just having fun playing with money and a real cash register. Now I know he was preparing me for life. Oh yeah, and I passed math.[35] **Tangent over.**

What if we treated our children's social and emotional learning the same way? What if, instead of being helicopter or snowplow parents, we practiced with them and prepared them for as many life situations as possible within the safe walls of the home, so when they get out into the real world, they are ready to handle anything life throws at them?

---

[35] That is…before they started putting letters in it.

# WHY YOU GOTTA BE SO RUDE?

One of the biggest things people want to know is, "Why are kids so mean? Why do they bully my kid? Or anyone's kid?" You are probably wondering that yourself. I love getting those questions because it allows me to take a very complicated issue and boil it down into simple, easy-to-understand terms.[36]

A great friend and colleague of mine, Brooks Gibbs, has researched this for years. He looked at all of the heady, academic, psychological studies and made it so anyone could understand. Brooks considered hundreds of years of psychological and sociological findings, including much of the work of famed psychologist Albert Ellis, and came up with the Aggression Trifecta - the three reasons people are mean to others.

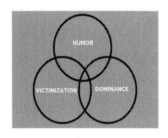

If you look at the diagram, it shows that all aggressive behavior fits into a combination of three categories: humor, victimization and dominance. Any conflict throughout history can be boiled down into this diagram, including one, two, or all three of these categories. Let's break this down a bit.

---

[36] What can I say? It's the teacher in me.

## *Humor*

Many times, people are mean to others because they think they are being funny. They are telling jokes about someone in an attempt to get a laugh. Everyone loves a good joke, but after studying and performing comedy for years, I can tell you that jokes are nothing more than pointing out the flaws of something or someone and bringing those flaws to the attention of others. The result is laughter. Think about any joke you've ever heard. There is always a "butt" to every joke. It's either a person or group of people, real or imaginary, an animal crossing the road, an object that doesn't work like it should...etc.

How many times have you heard a joke begin with, "How many blondes does it take to screw in a lightbulb?" Whatever the answer, the "butts" of the joke are blonde-haired people. Or, how about the classic, "Yo mama is so fat..." jokes? The "butt" of the joke is not only someone's mother, but also people who are overweight. And, the truth is, the bigger the "butt" of the joke, the funnier the joke tends to be. That's why, "Why did the chicken cross the road" is not very funny. But, videos showing little kids blindly swinging a baseball bat at a piñata and hitting their father in the groin by mistake are hilarious! Why do you think "fail" videos on Youtube are among the most popular? Why do you think *America's Funniest Home Videos* is ABC's longest running prime-time TV show? The bigger the "butt" of the joke, the funnier it is. It's just how humor works.

There are many times in our marriage where my wife laughs at me for one reason or another. Whether it's because I fell up the stairs, mixed up my words, or any one of the other million reasons there are to have a laugh at my expense, there is a great deal of laughter in our house. I'll never forget one occurrence in particular. I was walking into the kitchen, which I had done hundreds of times. Next to the kitchen entry was a small, wooden art table that our kids use for arts and crafts. For some reason, one day this table seemed to jump out from the corner and right into my path. I stubbed my little toe on the table leg, screamed like a baby, fell to my knees and tried to hold back the tears.[37] My wife thought it was the funniest thing in

---

[37] Don't laugh. You know that's the worst kind of pain next to child birth.

the world. While I was crying in pain, she was crying in laughter. Through the mist in my eyes, I managed to mutter one question: "Why are you laughing at me?!"

Trying to catch her breath, she answered, "I'm not laughing *at* you. I'm laughing *with* you."

"But I'm not laughing," I cried from the floor.

"Yes, but I am with you, and I'm laughing."

I can laugh about it now, but, whoo! My little piggy hurt so bad. But, I understand why it was so funny to my wife - funnier than almost any other situation I had found myself in up until that point. The "butt" of the humor was huge! It was so much funnier than a little slip of the tongue or a simple misstep in the house.

There are no jokes that are compliments. On the flip side, there are no compliments that are jokes. I once heard of a speaker who spoke to an audience of students and offered $10,000 to any kid that could come up with a funny compliment. No student could come up with anything…until…. One student came forward and said, "You walk up to a girl and say, 'Hey, nice mustache.'" The crowd laughed, of course and many thought the student had won the money. Unfortunately, he didn't. While it was a type of compliment, it was a backhanded compliment, also known as sarcasm. And, sarcasm is synonymous with mocking, ridicule, humor and joking.

The problem with humor is that the joke-teller may be innocently trying to get a laugh and have no malicious intent whatsoever. How many times have you scolded a child for saying or doing something and they responded with, "I was only kidding," or, "I didn't mean to hurt anyone." Now, I'm not naïve. I know full well that can often be a scapegoat excuse for someone trying to avoid punishment. But, there are many times where the joke was delivered out of innocence and the negative results were completely unintentional.

Here, many would say, "Well, that kid should know better than to make jokes about things that other people could be sensitive about." I agree. We are responsible for what comes out of our mouths. A little respect and forethought go a long way. We *should* teach children that some jokes may be hurtful to others and to exercise thoughtfulness in their words and actions. But, what if that only goes so far? What if they get tangled up in the wrong group for a moment? What if they have a momentary lapse of judgement, as kids tend to do? What if they abandon what they've been taught and make the decision to engage in making jokes about someone else? Heck, what if the kid rebels against authority, gets tattoos and piercings, colors his hair blue, consumes large amounts of gluten and totally ignores what his parents say?

The point is that nobody is perfect. We all have things that we wish we could change about ourselves. Maybe we can change them. Maybe we can't. Either way, there will always be people who point out our flaws and differences in order to get a laugh. Sometimes those things may be true. Sometimes they're exaggerated versions of the truth. Regardless, a resilient child is a child who has a strong sense of humor. All this implies is that they can understand when a joke is being told and, no matter the intent, be able to understand it as such and not be hurt by it. A psychologically and emotionally strong person can take a joke about themselves, process it as a joke, protect their feelings and brush it off, or even laugh about it. Walt Disney said, "To laugh at yourself is to love yourself."

To put icing on the cake, it also shows great strength to be able to add to the situation by inserting a joke about themselves when appropriate. This shows incredible resilience, self-confidence and self-esteem. The outcome? Your child will not be phased by jokes and, even if the jokester does have ill intent behind their humor, your child won't be a target for long because it's not fun to make jokes if the desired reaction isn't obtained.

Here's an example of how this could work:

Kid 1: *You're so fat, you have more rolls than a bakery.*

Kid 2: *Haha, that's a good one.*

Kid 1: *You probably get a group discount at a restaurant.*

Kid 2: {Laughing} *But, if there's ever a food shortage, I'm going to live the longest.*

Kid 1: *What?*

Kid 2: *It's ok, I know I'm big. I'm working on it, but for now, I'm blessed with this mess.*

Do you see how it works? It can be done with any joke about any topic. Once the aggressor sees that they are dealing with a resilient kid who cannot be hurt by jokes, the jokes will eventually stop and the victory belongs to your child.

So what can you do as parents and adults to help the next generation learn to deal with rude humor?

1. Help your children realize the fact that nobody is perfect, including them.

2. Change any negative thoughts they may have about themselves. Help them be able to accept their imperfections and be happy with who they are. If something can be done to change their circumstances (such as weight or hygiene), and they desire the change, great. Come up with a plan to work towards that change, making sure to keep self-esteem and self-confidence in tact.

3. Help them learn to laugh at themselves. Maybe even come up with some jokes about themselves to use as comebacks in a real life situation. Then, role play and help them practice the use of those comebacks to show their resilience.[38]

## *Victimization*

I'm sure we've all heard the phrase, "Hurting people hurt people." It's true. In fact, about 90% of kids that are labeled as "bullies" actually feel like victims in some area of their life before they engage in their aggressive behavior. The result? Anger, hatred

---

[38] Notice I said for your child to make jokes about themselves. Do not instruct them to make jokes about the aggressor. That will only make things worse and create a "one-up" situation.

and/or revenge. Anytime someone is acting out due to victimization, it is through anger, hatred, revenge, or a combination of the three. They are hurting and this is the only way they know how to deal with their hurt.

As I've said many times already, I'm not sticking up for the aggressor. They *should* know and understand that demeaning others and putting others down is not the way to get ahead in life, nor is it the proper way to deal with their issues. But, consider the psychology of a child or teen. What's going on in their minds? What's causing them to act the way they are?

Let's suppose that the "bully" is a kid that comes from a broken home or abusive family. Or, they may be the victim of a home where other unspeakable horrors have occurred. Maybe they are the victim of aggressive behavior in another part of their school life. They may feel like every teacher is against them. They may have some neighborhood peers that are harming them physically or emotionally. Maybe it's an issue of jealousy. Who knows?! There are tons of reasons someone can feel victimized. The point is, they are behaving with aggression towards others because that is how they are dealing with their feelings of victimization. It's one way of trying to get control over the emotional pain that exists in their life.

Many will then say, "Well, they should know better." Again, I agree. However, they haven't been taught how to handle their own victimization, so they are using aggression to cope. Did you catch that? Let me say it again. They haven't been **_TAUGHT_** how to properly deal with their own victimization, so they are using aggression towards others to help themselves cope.

Another possibility of the aggressive behavior is considering the fact that they may feel victimized by *your* child. Now, hang on. I'm not saying your child did something on purpose to harm someone else or cause ill feelings. But, sometimes the "bully" may feel anger, hatred or revenge towards your child because they feel that your child treated them unfairly. It could be that your child got them in trouble for something. Maybe there was a miscommunication between them that resulted in a bad test grade, relationship break up or an embarrassing cafeteria moment. Maybe something happened in gym class or recess that caused an accidental injury or damage to clothing or property. All of those things could easily be accidents, but in the mind of someone who feels like a victim, those things could easily be done on purpose as well.

After I explain this to parents, they usually ask the following: "But, why do they take it out on my kid? Why at school? Why on the bus?"

From my experience, the answer is two fold. First, they will act out in a location where they can get away with it. Second, it's usually because they feel a sense of safety. School, a certain class, and the bus may all feel like safe places for them – away from what is making them feel victimized – and they feel they can release their tension or act in such a way to level their own emotional playing field by making someone else feel like a victim.

So, what should you do? How can your child deal with someone who is choosing to deal with their victimization in this way? They are showing the classic signs of a victim: anger, hatred and/or revenge. They are hurting others because they feel victimized. Simple. *Apologize.*

**Hold up! What?! Boy, are you crazy?! I think you're crazy!**

I know it sounds crazy! Why should your child have to apologize for something that may not be their fault? Why should your child apologize for some other kid's rotten home life? It's not your child's fault. I get it. But, here's what happens: your child will show that they are not intimidated and genuinely caring about the other person's well-being. The result? Forgiveness, respect, civility, dare I say…friendship? Psychology is on your side here. Understand that getting defensive will only make the situation more tense and likely escalate it into something worse.

There's two key phrases to use to diffuse a situation. I've heard it called the Magic Response.

1. Are you mad?
2. I'm sorry.

Asking if the aggressor is mad allows the problem to be let out in the open. It also allows everyone involved to understand where the problem stems from, thereby paving the way for a proper apology.

The encounter may go down like this:

Aggressor: *Hey punk. I hate you. You're trash.*

Your child: (Gently) *What's going on? Is everything ok?*

Aggressor: *No, idiot.*

Your child: *Are you mad at me about something?*

Aggressor: *Yeah, fool. You got in my way and my milk spilled all over me.*

Your child: *Oh my goodness, I'm sorry. I was talking and didn't see you. It was an accident.*

Aggressor: *You ruined my favorite shirt.*

Your child: *I'm really sorry. I would never do that on purpose. I don't want any trouble. I'll be more careful.*

Aggressor: *You better.*

Your child: *I'm sorry. I will. Is there anything I can do to help?*

Chances are, that will resolve the conflict as long as your child maintains a calm, respectful tone the whole time.

But what if it's something that has nothing to do with your child, such as a home situation? Try this:

Aggressor: *Get out of the way punk!*

Your child: *Woah, is everything ok? Are you mad about something?*

Aggressor: *Who cares? Just get out of my way.*

Your child: *Ok. I'm sorry if you're having a rough day. I know how rough it is sometimes. I don't want to add to your bad day. If there's anything I can do, let me know.*

The more mature one should make an effort to apologize - even if they didn't do anything wrong. Don't apologize for a wrongdoing - or lack thereof. Simply apologize that they were wronged and feel victimized. Be legitimately sorry that they are having a rough day.

An ancient Jewish proverb says, "A gentle answer turns away wrath, but a harsh word stirs up anger."

In my humble opinion, I think every person in this country should work retail customer service. Why? Because in that environment, if you want to protect your own feelings, keep your sanity and hold onto your job, you have to learn how to deal with some pretty irate people. When I worked a retail job in college, I dealt with my fair share of customers who felt wronged by a company policy and decided to take it out on me and my co-workers; exhibiting anger, hatred and/or revenge. If I wanted to keep my job, I knew I needed to use some form of that Magic Response. I needed to calmly address the fact that the customer was upset, apologize for the fact that they felt wronged and then help to resolve the conflict for them. Now, sometimes, I wasn't able to give them the outcome they wanted and they left the store angry. But, they were not mad at me, in fact, they at least understood that I was not a threat to them or their happiness, and they were at least polite to me before they left.

**A gentle answer turns away anger, hatred and revenge.**

## *Dominance*

The third part of the Aggression Trifecta is dominance: one person is aggressive towards another because they want to exercise their control and power. They want to be top dog, king (or queen) of the mountain, big man (or woman) on campus. Their goal is to bother, annoy and drive someone crazy. As I said earlier, this is how most psychologists and sociologists classify "bullying:" dominance behavior.

Do you remember the game King of the Mountain? One kid stands on top of a hill while others run up the hill and try to push him or her down the hill to claim the title of king.[39] If your kids have ever played it, I'm sure you've seen your share of grass stains, dirt soils and ripped clothes. If you played it when you were a kid, I'm sure you remember the feeling of being on top of the hill. Even if it was just for a few seconds, it felt incredible to be king![40] Maybe you lasted up there for a while – throwing all of your challengers back down the hill one by one until the only way they could dethrone you was to team up and attack all at once.

"Bullying," by its psychological definition, is essentially the same thing as that old, favorite game. Psychologists refer to "bullying" as dominance behavior. A jostling for position. A desire to be top dog. Except, in the target's eyes, it's not really a game. When someone exhibits this behavior, it's usually to make themselves seem more powerful and establish themselves as dominant over someone else. This intentional bothering in an attempt to dominate is everywhere and it has been going on since the beginning of time. History is full of accounts of one person attempting to dominate another. Every single person has that innate need for dominance, to be the alpha, to survive, to win – especially if we are being threatened by someone else.

Who are the targets of this dominance behavior? I wish I could say there was a specific formula or profile for a kid who gets picked on. That would sure make things a lot easier. But, alas, there's not. Anyone can be a target at any time for any reason. Tall, short, skinny, overweight, glasses, braces, allergies, hair color, hair length, nervous ticks, hobbies, religious beliefs, sexuality, economic status, disabilities…anything! The fact is, if someone wants to exert his or her dominance over another student, they will find something, anything, to do it. Even if that something was never an issue before, they'll figure out a way to make it an issue. Whatever accomplishes the goal of dominance.

---

[39] Or queen.

[40] Or queen.

What's more? Parents want to know why – no – they **demand** to know why their children continue to be the targets of this type of behavior. How can the school sit back and do nothing? How can they just let it happen? How can they turn a blind eye to it?

Can I be honest? Remember, I'm your friend here. I'm in the same boat as you. I have kids. I'm a parent, too. Don't shoot the messenger. Remember what I said earlier: my teacher training has taught me that the best way to solve a problem is to look at it from all sides. So, let me frame this issue another way.

One of the first things to consider is where dominance behaviors typically occur the most. Study after study confirms that there is one place where dominance behaviors happen more than anywhere else. There is one place where name-calling, teasing, taunting, exclusion, pushing and shoving and that endless natural struggle for dominance happens more than anywhere. Here's a hint: it's not at school.

### *"Dang it, Chris! Quit beating around the bush! Tell me!"*

Ok, ok. It's in the home. Under your own roof. Sibling rivalry is the most common place for dominance behaviors to take place. If you are shocked by this you either:

A.  Have an only child, or
B.  Have some sort of wizard-like abilities to be able to have complete peace and harmony in your home at all times.

By the way, if your answer is B, you are missing out on billions of dollars from parents around the world who want to know your secret.

If your answer was neither A nor B, don't feel bad. Welcome to parenting. It's a psychologically proven fact, and makes perfect sense, that sibling rivalry is the most common setting of dominance behavior anywhere. Think about it. It's often true that those who are closest to us are the ones that can hurt us the most. They know our triggers. They know how to get under our skin. They know how to push every single button we have and get on every single, last nerve. And in most cases, they do it because, whether they realize it or not, it makes them feel like they are the top dog in the family. It fulfills that innate psychological need for dominance.

Siblings are no different. Throughout my career as a teacher, I've seen my share of sibling rivalries that spill over into the classroom. At one point, while directing a large middle school music performance group, I had an 8th grade boy named Thomas and his 6th grade sister Carly in the same class. They were part of a loving family. However, to say they were competitive would be an understatement. Even though they were two years apart, each attempted to dominate the other in music, sports, academics and popularity. Not a day went by that they weren't in competition with each other. Many times, this competition would arise during class and cause a stir. To be honest, it was pretty funny sometimes.

One day in particular, Thomas was being extra annoying in his 8th grade boy fashion. While playing his instrument, he was staring and making faces at Carly from across the room, trying to get her to mess up. Nothing else. Just staring and making faces. Carly looked up and saw. "Stop it!" she yelled.

Thomas responded, "I'm not doing anything." All the while keeping his heavily annoying eye contact.

She yelled back, "Quit it! You're so annoying! Ugh!" She raised her music stand higher so she could not see him.

What did Thomas do? He picked up his instrument, walked across the room while still playing, laid on the floor and began staring up at his sister. I'm not going to lie, it was pretty funny to watch. But by this point, Carly was fed up and done with Thomas's nonsense. Thomas, on the other hand, *knew* he was getting under her skin. He *knew* he was gaining an advantage over her and, once he found something that worked, he kept at it like Chinese water torture.

## *Under My Own Roof*

My daughter is two and a half years older than my son. It's a great thing, many times, to watch her teach him new things and pass on the wisdom that she's learned in her life. But, at the same time, she also tries to make sure he knows his place. She makes sure that he knows that he is the younger one, and he must submit to her authority. My son, on the other hand, will not take any of that nonsense. While he enjoys learning things from his older sister, and even looks up to her, in many ways he sees himself as an equal; sometimes even as dominant over her.

They both view themselves as a higher rank and more dominant. My daughter resorts to yelling to assert herself. In her mind, the louder she yells, the more power she has. My son, as boys tend to do, will use physical means — mostly pushing and smacking. Neither child wants to actually harm the other, but they want to get the point across that each is superior.

If you have more than one child, I'm willing to bet that your situation is very similar. Now, please understand that I'm not trying to make my house, or yours, sound like a constant battleground of screaming, hair pulling and attempted murder. Sure, there may be some verbal insults, physical tactics, pranks, etc. But, the goal is the same: dominate the others and be known as the boss; or in some cases, simply get some well-deserved respect.

What does this have to do with what your child is going through at school? It's no different. Some kid is exerting their dominance over your child and the result is hurt feelings, fear and intimidation. What happens next? Remember the Cycle of Aggression? It's going to happen over and over again because it makes the mean kid feel like a winner to watch your child get upset.

# EASY AS 1 - 2 - 3

So, by now I'm sure you're wondering if I'm just going to spend the whole book telling you what's wrong with schools and the anti-bully movement. "Will he ever tell me how to help my child?" Well, we're finally here.

As we've seen, it seems that mean, aggressive social behavior has become such a huge problem and nothing seems to be working. It just seems to keep getting worse. But, what if I told you that the solution is simple? What if I said that the answers have been right under our noses the whole time? Think I'm crazy? Just wait. Ready?

The solution to saving your child from their "bullying" problems is a simple three step process.

When I say that to people, I get some weird looks and even some that tell me I'm crazy. While many beg to know the three steps so they can try something different that may actually work for once, some talk to me quite condescendingly and tell me that there is no way a complex problem such as "bullying" can be solved so easily. I mean, if the problem is so big, huge and widespread, the solution has to be just as complicated. Right?

Nope. Just as with so many of life's problems, the best answer is often the simplest. Often times, thinking outside the box just means that we need to stop complicating things. Take a step back and look at things simply, from a different angle. For example:

Some people say the glass is half empty. Some say it's half full. This classic optimist vs. pessimist argument has been around for years. But, there is a third option that not many have considered. How about the fact that the glass is just too big? You see? When you change the way you look at things, the things you look at change.

Sit back, relax, open your mind and let's look at the steps together. Now, I will warn you that this way of thinking is different from what many schools and institutions are teaching. But, since we've already covered why those means are not working, let's think outside the box a bit and see what is actually working.

# STEP 1

## Think of "Bullying" As a Game

"Oh sure, let's just jump right out of the gates with the crazy! Bullying is a game? How can you say that? Bullying is nothing like a game! Kids are getting hurt! Lives are changed and scarred! How dare you!"

I'm sure that reflected the thoughts of some of you reading this. Rest assured, friends, I know how it sounds. But, before you shut this book, slam it down, throw it away and give me a bunch of 1 star reviews on Amazon, hang on. Let me explain. I'll say the statement again so you can read and process it properly.

Think of bullying as a game. ***Think of it*** as a game.

Remember, sound psychology teaches that when you change the way you look at things, the things you look at change. One of the first things a psychologist or counselor does with someone is help them reframe the problem. Put things in perspective. How can the problem be viewed differently so it doesn't seem as scary and insurmountable? *Think* of it as a game.

Children understand games easily, and framing the problem like a game works quite well for children of all ages. It makes things easier to handle mentally and emotionally. They understand that, in games, there are winners and losers. Nobody likes to lose. It's no fun. And, nobody wants to play a game they know they are going to lose. But, if you have a chance of winning, you may be more willing to play. What's more, if you know that you are guaranteed victory, it's no problem to go out and claim it.

That's how "bullies" see things; as a game. Remember the Cycle of Aggression? That's the game! It makes them feel like a winner to make your child feel like a loser. They know they will win every time, so they continue to play the game. Your child, however, keeps getting dragged into a game that they have no idea how to get out of. No idea how to win.

Don't lose heart, though. Because just like every other game, there is a strategy for your child to win, too. You just have to find it. Through the right coaching and understanding how the game works, a winning strategy is only two more steps away.

Every time a student has come to me with a social issue, the conversation usually goes like this:

Me: *When that kid makes fun of you, does it make you feel good or bad?*

Student: *Bad.*

Me: *Does it make you feel like a winner or a loser?*

Student: *A loser.*

Me: *How do you think it makes them feel? Like a winner or a loser?*

Student: *They feel like a winner.*

Me: *What if I told you there was a way you could win?*

Student: *Beat him up?*

Me: *Haha, no. But do you want to know how to win every time so they eventually leave you alone?*

Student: *Yes, please!*

# STEP 2

## Don't Get Upset

### _Resilience_

I'm not so sure we have a "bullying" problem in this country as much as we have a _resilience_ problem. Let me explain.

Which of these two things has changed the most over the last 30 years: the fact that people are mean, or the resilience/frustration levels of people? From everything I've seen, the biggest change has come from a drastic reduction of resilience and frustration tolerance - and I'm not just talking about kids. If you take an honest look at society, it's easy to see that people are getting upset, hurt and offended easier than ever before. Yes, people have been hurt in the past. Yes, things are a bit different now with the internet, apps and online avenues allowing people the anonymity and behind-screen courage to say things they normally wouldn't. But, again, if we're honest, the lack of resilience is the biggest change.

Resilience is the ability for people to bounce back after going through a difficult time. Being resilient just means being able to get back up after you've been knocked down. Being able to bounce back stronger than you were before. Being able to go through some stress, adversity, junk and deal with some haters and emerge stronger than ever. Resilient people can go through stress and adversity and come out unscathed. Or, as I tell the kindergarteners, resilience simply means to be strong.

Resilient kids are bully-proof. Resilient kids are able to understand and accept the fact that they are not perfect, and neither is anyone else. Resilient people are nearly impossible to offend. Resilient people are able to laugh at themselves. Resilient people are able to brush off insults, be happy with a handful of *true* friends, accept the fact that they may not be invited to every gathering, and not get upset by a push or shove that doesn't cause pain.

Resilience is a learned trait. We're not born with it. Children must be taught to be resilient. How? First, it starts with understanding the fact that life will not always go their way. There will always be mean people. There will always be someone who laughs, makes a joke, teases, spreads a rumor, excludes them or does something make them upset. We, as adults, understand that fact…I hope. Not all kids do, yet.

Now, there are many that will read that and say something like, "Yeah. I tell my kid 'Suck it up, buttercup, and deal with it.'" While that may be what you *want* to say, it's not the best way to word it. Consider your audience. A hurting child, no matter the age, does not want to be met with, "Just suck it up." Instead, find those teachable moments in their lives where you can have those heart-to-heart conversations and provide the wisdom and understanding that only you can. Not only will they be better off, but it will help grow your relationship with them. If you want to be proactive, start having those discussions before the hurt happens.

How awesome would it be if all of our kids were mentally tough and emotionally strong? How awesome would it be if our kids could be so resilient, so strong, that no matter what anyone ever said to them it would bounce right off and not affect them in the slightest bit? But, so many people, not just kids, live with paper thin skin and their emotions on their sleeves that if someone even looks at them the wrong way they fly off the handle, loose their cool and their world comes crashing down.[41] In my opinion, the number one threat to your child's academic success, their leadership influence and their influence with their peers is their ability, or inability, to control their own thoughts, emotions and reactions.

---

[41] You're probably thinking of someone who fits that description right now.

## *ABC's*

There are a spectrum of emotions that every person can experience at any given point. To make things simple, let's focus on the 4 big ones: anger, sadness, neutral, and happiness. When we experience the different facets of life, we feel some semblance of these emotions. And so often, we say things like, "Oh, that makes me so happy." "That person just makes me incredibly angry!" "I don't really care either way." "You made me really sad." Notice the language there - and the language we all use when we express our emotions. *That* makes me happy. *That person* makes me angry. *You* made me sad. We live by the notion that other people and outside circumstances determine our feelings and emotions. We put the blame on them. Dr. Albert Ellis proved that to be incorrect.

Through his work, Dr. Ellis found that people's interactions with other people and situations follow an A-B-C pattern. Simply put, we experience an **activating event**; A. Life. Things happen to us, big and small. We interact with people who are nice and people who are mean. We cannot control those things. They just happen.

The next thing that we see or notice is our emotional **consequence**; C. This is our reaction to the activating event. We get mad. We become sad. We have neutral feelings or don't really care. We're happy. We have an emotional response to the things and people we come in contact with.

You're probably thinking, "Wait a second. That sounds right, but where's the B? What's the B? When's the B?" The crazy part is, this is the biggest part of the equation, but it happens within a split second almost unconsciously. The B stands for your **beliefs**. Each of us has a set of things we believe, and our beliefs determine how we interpret the situation. From there, we create our feelings about the things we encounter. Dr. Ellis discovered that it's not the actual event or person that causes us to be angry, sad, neutral or happy. It's how we interpret things based on our beliefs.[42]

Think about it. Someone flips you the middle finger in traffic (A). And because you believe that the middle finger is a horrible

---

[42] https://www.simplypsychology.org/cognitive-therapy.html

insult and nobody has the right to do that to you (B), you get angry and flip them the middle finger, too (C).

Let's change the narrative a bit. Someone flips you the middle finger in traffic (A). But, because you don't really get offended by the middle finger and other insults (B), you go about your day as if it didn't happen taking care to be more careful next time you need to change lanes (C).

Now, put that in perspective with what your child may be going through. Someone calls your child a name (A). Because your child thinks that words always hurt and everyone *must* be kind to them (B), your child's day is ruined (C).

Let's change the narrative. Let's say you've been working with your child so that they aren't easily upset by words and insults. Someone calls them a name (A). Because your child is resilient and understands that words don't have to hurt (B), they are able to shake it off or even laugh it off, and have a great day regardless of what someone said to them (C).

Bookstores and libraries are filled with books about mindset. Business leaders, psychologists and self-help gurus have penned many works detailing how changing one's thinking can change the outcome of situations. It's a psychologically-proven tactic. You can train your brain to think differently about things, thereby changing your emotional outcome. What's that mean? We can train our kids to change the emotional outcome of their situations by helping them change the way they think about words, insults, jokes and aggressive situations.

## *It's Not a Lie*

There's an old saying that I love. You've probably heard it. It's quite fitting for what we're talking about.

**Sticks and stones may break my bones but words will never hurt me.**

I said that in a school recently and one kid called out from the back of the room, "Unless someone throws a dictionary at you!"

The entire auditorium erupted in laughter. And I did, too. It was hilarious! I guess that is a case in which words *can* hurt you.

Anyway, when people hear that I teach "Sticks and Stones" as a way to deal with mean people, they often want to say that it's a lie. I've read numerous articles, headlines, and billboards that claim that "Sticks and Stones" is a lie and we need to stop using it. However, once they know the origins of the saying, they are quick to rethink their position.

The slogan dates back to the mid 1800's with the African American slaves. In the early 1860's, they knew freedom was within reach. They knew Lincoln was going to set them free. But, they also knew that, as they went out into the real world as free citizens, they were going to encounter some mean, hateful people. They weren't naive. They just knew that there were some mean people in the world. So, an African Methodist Episcopal church began publishing this old adage: *Sticks and stones may break my bones, but words will never break me.* It stuck and has survived for hundreds of years.

Here's the truth. The slaves knew that if someone hit them with a stick or a stone, it would hurt. It could break their bones. There was nothing they could do to change that end result. However, they understood that each person has the power to control whether or not words hurt them. They knew they would be called the "N" word. They knew they would be called every name in the book. They knew it! But they made the decision that they would not let the negative words of anyone get to them. They understood that they had control over their thoughts, emotions and reactions. They knew that **words only have the power that the listener gives them.**

Whenever someone challenges me on this, I ask them if they'd rather be punched in the face or called an idiot. They have to choose one. They always say they'd rather be called an idiot. So, of course, I ask why. Every person answers just the way you'd imagine. "Because a punch would hurt, but being called an idiot doesn't have to bother me."

Don't get me wrong. I know that words *can* sometimes hurt. I've been upset and hurt by words just as much as the next guy. But they don't have to hurt. Maybe a better way to word it would be:

Sticks and stones may break my bones, but words **don't have to hurt me.**

You see, friends, when you say things like that to yourself and your child repeatedly, it starts to stick. It becomes a coping skill, which we'll talk about later. It doesn't matter what is said, how many times it's said or who says it. Words only have the power that the listener gives them. When your child understands and believes that, they win.

### *Why Me?!*

Parents often ask, "Why is *my* kid picked on more than others?" It's a completely valid question. Many times, there are other children in class, on the team or in the same environment that have the same features, quirks and distinctions, but they are left alone. Why? Why can there be dozens of overweight kids in a school, but only one or two are teased constantly? Why can there be so many kids who lack athletic ability in gym class, but only one is made fun of every day?

If you haven't picked up on the theme yet, I'd venture to say that, based on my experience, it's based on one thing: resilience. Resilience is the separator. Resilient people are able to manage their emotions. Because they're not phased by much, they are able to keep an even keel and a level head. We all know people who are resilient and people who aren't. Throughout his decades of research and treatment of patients, Dr. Albert Ellis determined that people who lack resilience have thoughts such as these:

*"I must perform well and receive approval from important people. Otherwise, I am a failure."*

*"Every person must treat me fairly and protect me from pain. Otherwise, they should be punished."*

*"Life must be comfortable and give me what I want. Otherwise, life is unbearable."*

Did you catch the strong language in those thoughts? It's from one word. **_Must._** These are demands. Absolutes with a strong sense of entitlement. Do you see how this type of thinking can lead to problems down the road? When these demands aren't met, things can get ugly. People who think these thoughts:

- Cannot accept anything less than perfection from themselves and others
- Blame others for their negative circumstances
- Don't take responsibility for their actions
- Tend to be very sore losers
- Usually always have a victimization mindset
- Constantly seek approval from others
- Think nobody likes them and/or everyone hates them
- Don't do well with change
- Have a low self-esteem
- Have low self-confidence
- Use absolutes such as "Must" and "Never"
- Have unhealthy coping skills
- Are quick to anger and frustration
- Have a greater risk for depression
- Either explode, implode or shut down in the face of adversity
- Buckle under stress
- Are often at a greater risk for health issues
- ...and so much more

I'm sure you are thinking about someone who fits those descriptions right now. If so, heres a question: Do you enjoy hanging out with that person? My guess is probably not. They probably have a negative outlook on life, tend to always be on edge and have learned to walk around with an Eeyore-type of mentality.

Now, take a second to reflect on that list again. How does your child/children match up? Some of you have no worries at all because none of those things apply to your kids. Some of you may be scared out of your wits because your child met most or every one of those characteristics. The main reason certain students seem to have targets on their backs while other students with similar characteristics are left alone is because of the way they respond to adversity, stress and mean behavior. As we'll see in a bit, the response to mean behavior can almost always dictate what happens next.

To understand this, you have to understand the Law of Reciprocity.

## It's The Law

The Law of Reciprocity says that you treat others the same way they treat you. If someone is nice to you, you're nice back. Think about the last time someone complimented you. Maybe they said something nice about your hair, your clothes, your children or a job you did. I'm willing to bet it made you feel good. Possibly even great! A good, uplifting word can often be stored away in your memory bank and pulled back out on a rough day to help brighten things.

However, reciprocity works the other way, too. If someone is mean to you, it almost seems natural to have ill feelings toward them in return. In many cases, you may even throw an insult right back in retaliation, possibly even worse than the one they said to you. And then you think to yourself, "How dare they say that to me! They don't know who they're dealing with! They wanna see crazy? I'll show 'em crazy!"

Throughout my career, I heard many squabbles begin with something as simple as this:

Kid 1: Your face is ugly.

Kid 2: Shut up! Your mom is ugly!

From there, things would escalate.

That's reciprocity. It's one thing humans have in common with animals. When an animal feels threatened, what does it do? The fangs come out, the claws spread apart, the animals assumes its most intimidating position and gets ready to attack. When humans feel threatened, we act very similarly, often in a very mirror-like, or reciprocal way to the aggression against us. Don't believe me? Go watch a video of two gorillas getting into a fight, and then head down to your local tavern and watch two macho blockheads disagree over who saw the girl first. The two situations will look fairly similar.[43] The reason for this is because humans and animals have a similar brain structure.

**Warning: If you are easily bored with heady, technical jargon, skip ahead. If you want a quick synopsis of the similarities and differences between a human and animal brain, continue. I'll make it as painless as possible.**

Ok, brave friends. Here we go. When faced with a stressful, dangerous or high-tension situation, we either run away or we go into beast mode, puff up and prepare to attack back with equal or greater force. It's one of the things we have in common with the animal kingdom. The part of the brain where this happens is called the amygdala, which is part of the limbic system. In simple terms, this is the emotional center of the brain.

Humans, however, are a bit different than animals.[44] But in terms of the brain, humans differ quite a bit from animals. The human cerebral cortex allows for us to have a higher level of reasoning. We are able to make decisions, weigh pros and cons, anticipate consequences and so forth. Most animals are not able to do so due to the differences in our brains.

Any basic, introductory psychology class will teach this basic fact: that people are in charge of their own thoughts, feelings, emotions and reactions. Granted, it is, at times, difficult and not part of our natural fight or flight instinct. But ultimately, due to the cerebral cortex, humans are able to control their thoughts, emotions and reactions to situations. Not only that, but it is socially expected

---

[43] Except the two barflies will be much less intimidating than the gorillas.

[44] I say "a bit" knowing that we all have that one person in our lives whose eating habits, sleeping habits, personality or hygiene practices more resemble those of animals.

that each person be able to do so and accept responsibility for those things.

**If you skipped ahead, welcome back.**

Psychology teaches that we are the masters of our own emotions. We don't have to get angry or upset. We process how other people treat us and we decide to get upset. So, the key is to refrain from getting upset. Teach your child to refuse to get upset. Don't let the words, rumors, rejection, laughter, jokes, etc. hurt them. If "bullying" is a game, and it makes the mean kid feel like a winner to make your child upset, teach your child to protect their feelings, guard their heart and find ways to build their self-esteem and confidence. To put it another way:

*In order for someone to break your heart, they have to go through your brain.*

The key towards making this work is helping your child understand this fact:

*There will always be mean people and you cannot control them.*

It's true. I'm sure we've all driven ourselves crazy at some point by trying to turn someone else into something they're not. We've tried to force someone to be something they're not, especially if they are not willing to change. The world isn't always going to be sunshine, rainbows and unicorns and things aren't always going to go their way. But, it's ok.

The key to being strong and resilient is not to hide from adversity. Strength is only gained by going through adversity. It's like building a muscle. Anyone trying to get strong and build muscle isn't going to the gym every day and lifting feathers. They lift weights and they increase the weight over time. They put their bodies through stress and, through that stress, they get stronger. Strength is only built by working through resistance. What's the benefit of working out and getting stronger? Besides being more fit and healthy, you are more independent and able to accomplish more tasks on your own. Pretty soon, there isn't a pickle jar in the world that will stay shut.

The cool thing about emotional resilience, though, is that it can be taught. The more our emotional "muscles" get taught how to properly operate, the stronger they get. What's the result? Mental and emotional strength enabling you to solve problems on your own with thick skin, a clear head, and a pure and protected heart.

But, how do you help a child make that switch? How do you get them to go from anger and sadness to neutral feelings? Even more, how can we get them to have a positive outlook on the situation? Can they actually be glad it happened and see the learning opportunities at hand? Through years of painstaking research, my friend and sociologist Brooks Gibbs has boiled it down into three points.

First, help them see how could it be worse. By asking a child to compare their negative situation to the worst case scenario, they can start to see that their temporary social problem is not the worst thing in the world. It's actually a coping mechanism that we, as adults, use on a regular basis. Want proof? Anytime someone is in a fender bender, one of the first things said is, "It could've been a lot worse." Anytime there is a storm, flood, or some type of disaster, people always find a reason to say, "It could have been worse." It helps us put things into perspective and start to see things on the bright side.

Second, to further put things into perspective, help them see that this current squabble will likely not even matter in the future. A very successful businessman once told me, "If it's not going to matter in 5 years, I forget it and move on." Think about your own life. How many times have you said something like, "Well, I'm not going to see her ever again, so I don't care." The same goes for our kids. Will this situation, insult, disagreement, etc. matter 5 years from now? Is this one incident truly going to effect who they are and what they will become down the road? If you can help your child get to a "no" for that question, it diminishes the importance of the situation and helps them get past the hurt and anger much quicker.

Lastly, ask your child to think of ways to see things in a positive light. How could this actually be a good thing? What can be learned from this? How can this actually be beneficial moving forward? This one is a bit tricky. Sometimes it's very difficult to see the the good in the bad. But, trust me, it's there.

In early 2019, I was blessed to spend a week in Moore, Oklahoma visiting a number of schools, speaking to students, parents and teachers. If you're not familiar with Moore, it is a town of about 60,000 people just south of Oklahoma City.[45] Over the years, Moore has been hit with a great deal of tornadoes, especially those in the EF-4 to EF-5 range. Most recently, a devastating EF-5 twister ravaged a great deal of the town in May of 2013 leaving 24 dead, over 200 injured and causing over $2 billion worth of damage to this incredible town. During my visit, I heard the stories of what it was like in the schools the day the tornado hit.

In the aftermath, however, the attitude of the citizens of Moore was staggering. They became the epitome of resilience. Six years after the tragedy, they are still looking on the bright side, speaking life and hope. They used that event to improve the entire city. One of the schools rebuilt their gym into a state-of-the-art tornado shelter. Everyone in the town now knows an exact plan of what to do if something like that ever happens again. Emergency crews are more prepared. Families hug each other tighter. Relationships are valued more. There is a sense of unity in Moore that I can't say I've seen in many other places. What a way to look at life! If the amazing people of Moore can find good in a horrific tragedy, I'm convinced that anyone can find good in any situation.

When your child can work through these steps and exhibit resilience, they begin to tip the scales back into their favor. They level the playing field. When they can look in the mirror and say, "I'm happy with who I am and how I am, and I don't care what anyone says about me," they win! What happens next? They realize they *can* do it so it increases their self-esteem and self-confidence, and they are much more prepared for the next time a situation rises.

Before resilience is taught and implemented, the encounter may go something like this:

---

[45] It's also the hometown of country music star Toby Keith.

Mean kid: *You're such an idiot.*

Your child: *Shut up. Leave me alone!*

Mean kid: {seeing they now have the upper hand} *You're a freak.*

Your child: {getting more upset} *Leave me alone! Stop it!*

Mean kid: {feeling like a winner} *What are you gonna do about it, freak?*

And it escalates from there.

But, when your child is resilient and understands steps 1 and 2, the conflict looks very different:

Mean kid: *You're such an idiot.*

Your child: {calmly} *That's nice.*

Mean kid: {slightly confused} *You're a freak.*

Your child: {shrugging it off} *Sorry you feel that way.*

Mean kid: {intensifying while realizing they are having no effect on your child} *You smell like armpits and puke! You're so nasty!*

Your child: {still calm} *Thanks for the info. I'll try a new deodorant.*

Mean kid: {seeing they're getting nowhere} *You should just go kill yourself.*[46]

Your child: {still calm} *Nah, I'd miss you too much, Buttercup!*

Rest assured that by this point the conflict should be over. But, there's one more step. Let's put the icing on the cake.

---

[46] Yes, that's an actual insult that kids are saying to each other these days.

# STEP 3

### Live the Golden Rule

We all know the Golden Rule. We've been taught it since Kindergarten.

### *Treat others the way you want to be treated.*

Everywhere I go and teach this, I hear the same thing: "We already teach the Golden Rule. We have posters everywhere. We reinforce it daily. How is your method any different?" I'm always happy they ask.

Wouldn't the world be so much better if we all lived by the Golden Rule? Silly question. Of course it would. Aristotle noted that if everyone lived by the Golden Rule, we wouldn't need government or police. But, alas, we don't live that way. On the contrary, we live by the law of reciprocity; the opposite of the Golden Rule.

I'll never forget one mother who attended a parent event that was hosted by a school. I began my spiel about the Golden Rule and she piped up, "Yeah! Tell that to the punks who are picking on my kid! They need to treat people the way they want to be treated!"

I'm sure her child's aggressors had heard the Golden Rule before; probably thousands of times. For years we've been focusing on the mean kids, telling them, "Hey, treat people how you want to be treated. Stop being mean. Be nice." And, that is important. Kids need constant reminders of what types of behaviors are acceptable and unacceptable. However, for all the years we've been telling the mean kids to be nice, the targets have been sitting back and praying that the message would finally hit its mark. And, for as many times as the message has been preached, the mean behavior is still happening.

But, what if we turn to the targets and teach them how the Golden Rule can work **in their favor?** What if we teach kids the difference between reciprocity and the Golden Rule? What if we teach kids how to properly ***respond*** to mean behavior, as opposed to ***reacting*** and allowing reciprocity to take over. That secret lies within the Golden Rule.

### *Reacting vs. Responding*

When I work with students on their social issues, I share something I learned in pre-marital counseling. The pastor, married to the same woman for 40+ years, sat across from my soon-to-be wife and I, looked us in the eyes and gave us this golden nugget: If you're in an argument, **the first one to yell, loses.** It's a sign that you have lost control of yourself. In your child's situation, that one fact could mean the difference between the mean behavior stopping or getting worse.

I've shared that with countless students throughout my teaching career, and now as a speaker with hundreds of thousands of students around the country each year. It's a simple fact that can help them remember the difference between reacting vs. responding.

Reacting is emotional. It's instinctual. It's not calculated. It's uncontrollable. Knee-jerk, if you will. Think of a chemical reaction. Vinegar and baking soda. It's going to bubble over. That's the reaction. It's just what happens.

Responding, however, is different. A response is planned and thought-out. It often works against instinct and allows for careful consideration. Many school tests no longer require "answers," but rather "responses." "Short answer" questions are now called "brief response." "Multiple choice answers" are now called "selective response." "Essay answers" are now called "extended response." The simple switch in verbiage communicates the fact that teachers want student's to carefully think through their work.

While the home is certainly the most common place for dominance behavior and aggression, it's also the biggest training ground for your kids to learn how to deal with the haters of the world who would treat them poorly. I teach my own kids the simple, yet important, truth that some people are just going to be mean; including their siblings. You can't control other people or how they treat you, but you can control how you respond to them. My daughter can't control if my son treats her poorly, but she can control her response. Her response will then dictate his next move. If she gets mad and reacts in kind, we'll have a nasty situation on our hands. But, if she controls her thoughts and emotions, and responds in a respectful manner, my son will be more likely to stop his mean behavior and the conflict will end.

## *Joey*

In my first book, *P.S. I Bully U*, I shared a story about a student I once taught named Joey.[47] Joey was in seventh grade when I had him in my class. We were in a small school in western Texas. If memory serves, there were about 80 students spanning grades kindergarten through 8th. Joey was much shorter than everyone else in his grade. There was nothing physically wrong with him. He just hadn't hit his teenage growth spirts yet. His blonde hair, soft eyes and gentle tone of voice made Joey seem like a sweet kid. And he was, for the most part.

Everybody loved to pick on Joey. Why? Because Joey had a nasty temper. Any time he would get mad, it was like the fourth of July. Fireworks! Tears. Red face. Screaming. Crying. I witnessed Joey throw desks, chairs, sporting equipment and anything else he could get his hands on. He would attack others. Once, I caught him sitting in a corner ripping out his own hair.[48] And the other kids

---

[47] I also share it with select live audiences.

[48] Please note, there was nothing emotionally or mentally wrong with Joey. He was tested.

loved it! They loved knowing the fact that they had the power to make Joey upset. It even got to the point where some kindergarteners would pick on seventh grade Joey because they knew they could control what happened today on the "Joey Show."

One day, during my class, I turned to write something on the board. As I was doing so, someone whispered something to Joey that caused him to get upset. Joey stood up and flipped his desk over. Papers flew everywhere. Next, he picked up his chair and threw it against the wall. After that, he ran out of the classroom, down the hall and out the front door of the building. Everyone in the room was frozen.

I ran outside to try and find him, but I couldn't. Any adult understands that when you are missing a child, 10 seconds is an eternity. I was running around the parking lot screaming his name. Nothing. I looked under cars. I couldn't find him. I was thinking the worst. I was afraid I was going to lose my job. I was afraid that Joey was going to run away, be kidnapped, or get hit by a car. I was terrified.

Nearly 30 seconds later, Joey emerged from behind some bushes next to the building. He was running, flailing his arms frantically, screaming and crying. Once I finally got him to calm down, he told me what happened. Apparently, another student, with whom Joey had previous negative encounters, made some very nasty comments. Joey got upset, ran outside and sat behind the bushes to cry. However, in doing so, he unknowingly sat on top of a fire ant hill.

That day, Joey finally learned how his reactions were fueling the negative behaviors against him. The more he reacted, the more others would treat him poorly. However, after that incident, he realized he needed to listen to his teachers and adult mentors who had been desperately trying to help him with positive ways of dealing with negative situations.

## _Update on Joey_

So many people were angry with me after reading the chapter about Joey in _P.S. I Bully U._ How did Joey turn out? What happened after the fire ant incident?

Joey grew up. He went from being one of the shortest in his class to over 6 feet tall. He gradually learned positive coping skills and resilience strategies. He graduated high school and went on to work in his father's construction business where he is a project manager. At any one time, he leads a crew of 5 or more workers, all the while gaining leadership experience. Last I heard, he was hoping to take over the business after his father retired. Happy ending.

## _A New Perspective_

While the Golden Rule is very widely taught, I don't think its full wisdom is wholly taught.

The Golden Rule is ancient. It's over 3000 years old, dating back to Aristotle who taught, "Whatever you hate, don't do to someone." To this day, almost every major religion has their own version of the Golden Rule. Now, many people think that Jesus invented the Golden Rule. He didn't, however he was the first one to put in positive language. Rather than using words like "don't" and "hate," Jesus said, "Do unto others and as you have them do unto you." Same message, worded a bit more positively.

I think we need to word the Golden Rule this way:

**Treat others the way you want to be treated, _no matter how they treat you first._**

That last caveat is the missing link that communicates the _full_ wisdom of that ancient gem. It implies the simple fact that there will always be mean people and the way to deal with them is to treat them the way you want to be treated.

At this point, I usually ask kids, "How do you want to be treated? Like a friend, or an enemy?" Every student I ask replies that they want to be treated like a friend, not an enemy. Nobody wants more enemies. So, the simple solution is to treat everyone like a friend, even your enemies.

Again, when some people hear this they think I'm crazy. I'm often met with, "You must be crazy! My kid is the target and they're supposed to be nice back?!"

"Yup," I respond.

"That doesn't make any sense," they quip.

It does if you understand the Golden Rule. Dr. Martin Luther King, Jr. said, "You cannot drive out hate with more hate, only love can do that." What was he saying? Use the Golden Rule against your enemies! It will, ultimately, stop the hate.

Abraham Lincoln said, "Do I not destroy my enemies when I make them my friends?" Again, the Golden Rule. It is the secret to transform enemies into friends. If not that extreme, it will at least bring the relationship back to neutral, respectable grounds. When you make the conscious decision and effort to take control of your reactions and use the Golden Rule to combat the negativity of others, a few things begin to happen:

1. You gain back control of yourself. You are no longer a puppet in the game of your aggressors.

2. You gain control of the situation. They are expecting you to react a certain way. By not doing so, they are thrown off guard, giving you the upper hand. The ball is in your court.

3. You start to win the game every time.

By treating a mean person the way you want to be treated, it takes that Law of Reciprocity and flips it around to work in your favor instead of against you. If peoples' natural instinct is to mirror others' treatment of them, let's use it for good. Use it to stop the mean behavior that's being thrown at you.

In the appendix of this book, you'll find instructions for a simple game that you can play with your child to illustrate how the

Golden Rule works. I call it "Stop It." I encourage you to play it with your child and watch the lightbulb flip on once they see how simple it really is.

# PUTTING IT ALL TOGETHER

Putting all of this information together is like any game involving strategy. Let's say football. Wouldn't it be nice to know the other team's playbook? It would be like getting inside the heads of the players, knowing exactly what would happen and when so then you could plan your defense and offense to win the game. It's the same thing here.

First, determine what their play is. What happened? Use specific language. The words "bully" and "bullying" are off limits. Did the mean person say something mean to your child? Did they do something mean? Did they say something to someone else about your child? Did they exclude your child?

Next, determine why the behavior happened? Listen to your child's full side of the story, uninterrupted. Does it sound like the aggressor was simply telling a joke, just trying to get a laugh? Does it sound like they are acting out at your child because they feel hurt in some way? Or, does it sound like they are trying to bother your child to get a reaction and exert dominance? Note: There may be one or more reasons at play. For example, because they feel hurt for some reason, the aggressor may be using jokes in order to upset your child.

Ok, so we know the play. What's the defense? Resilience. Your child knows the mean behavior is coming. They can mentally and emotionally prepare for what's coming. And, using proper coping skills which we'll discuss later, they can guard their heart, realize that they are able to win the game and become mentally and emotionally invincible. Stay calm. Don't get upset.

The offense? The Golden Rule. Responding rather than reacting. Maybe laughing is the proper response. Maybe an apology will squelch the conflict. Perhaps just responding with kindness as opposed to reacting in reciprocity will turn things around. Regardless of what it looks like, use the Golden Rule. The goal is not to create enemies. The goal is to, at the very least, stop the conflict before it gets out of hand.

# YEAH, BUT WHAT IF...

Sometimes, parents say, "But, Chris, what if my child is not witty or quick to think of snappy comebacks." Or, sometimes I hear, "My child has special needs or Autism and they don't have the social awareness or skills to handle a situation like that. What do I teach them?"

I'm going out on a limb here, so bear with me. It's a great question. Children with special needs are awesome. As a teacher, they were some of my favorites to work with. Anywhere from Down's Syndrome to all along the Autism spectrum, and everything in between, each child's skills, abilities and needs are different. However, there is one generally common thread between all of them: the development of their social skills.

For many of these children, their social skills take a very long time to mature, if they ever do. Simple things that you and I may take for granted - eye contact, holding a conversation, and acknowledging social cues like humor and sarcasm - may take many years to develop. Some kids see the good in everyone. They love people and everything about life. They have a sweet, innocent naivety that melts your heart. They don't have a mean bone in their body and they don't really understand meanness or sarcasm.

My first year of teaching was highlighted by a class of 6 special education students. I so looked forward to Thursdays at 1:00 PM when I got to see them. As a music teacher, I got to see their faces light up when I would strum a guitar chord, play a song on the piano or give them a tambourine.

I'll never forget Tavon. On the Autism spectrum, Tavon was fairly high-functioning, but not enough for a mainstream, on-level classes. Tavon loved everyone! His goal was to make everyone as happy as he was. It didn't matter who, when or how, he would always smile and say, "Hi." As part of his social learning protocol, Tavon had to move past just greeting people and work on giving compliments. It didn't take long before he was a pro. Every day, I'd pass him in the hallway and he'd say, "Hi, Mr. Scheufele! I like your shirt." "Good morning, Mr Scheufele. I like your hair." I almost lost it one day when I was walking down the hall eating an apple. As I passed Tavon, he smiled and confidently said, "Hi, Mr. Scheufele! I like your apple!"

Tavon rarely got upset or in trouble. When his teacher was angry, he had trouble processing negative emotions because everything about his life was always fun and smiles. It wasn't until someone raised their voice that he would understand that something was wrong. However, he wasn't always sure how to respond, so he would cower or cry.

Then there's the other end of the spectrum. Some kids are emotionally unstable at all times; loose cannons. They have no filter. They don't know, or care, about their surroundings or the well-being of others. Few things hold their attention or make them happy. Anything outside of that and the results are unpredictable.

Brody was an interesting child. Mildly functional on the autism spectrum, he was generally a good kid, with a good heart. But, he had a temper and the mouth of a sailor. He didn't care who was around or how many adults tried to teach him to censor his foul language, he spoke his mind. He lived by reciprocity. In fact, he would even try to one-up anyone who offended him - often to the point of taking things too far. Brody was one of the most suspended students in school. It seemed like he was always in trouble for pulling another kid's hair or biting. He would make sure to have the last word or deed.

For the most part, he only understood and expressed negative emotions. It seemed that the only way to make Brody happy was to give him a video game, Pokemon cards or to make everything about him right that very second. He didn't understand sarcasm or jokes. He took everything negatively and literally, and he was quick to let you know how he felt about it.

Both Tavon and Brody had trouble with social cues and social emotional learning. They both had social skills worked into their Individual Education Plan (IEP). Neither was able to really take a joke. Neither was able to properly respond to negative behavior. So, how were they supposed survive a "bullying" situation?[49] Someone like Tavon would have no idea what was happening until things got so bad he crumbled. A child like Brody would try to smash the other kid's face at the mere utterance of a cross word.

The easiest and most effective way for children with any type of learning difference (or even those who are too young to know better), is to teach them how to respond. Simple quick responses can be taught and memorized extremely easily. And, even if they can't be memorized, they can at least fit on a small wallet-sized card to be kept hidden away until needed.

### The Responses

There are basically two responses that I teach kids to use. Each one is short, easy to memorize and can be used over and over again.

**Response number one**: *Haha, you're funny. You should be a comedian.*

The power behind this is three-fold. First, it shows resilience. It's nearly impossible to say without smiling, and it shows the aggressor that their mean words were taken as a joke - which is most likely the complete opposite of what they want.

---

[49] I know, I know! The fact that someone would pick on a child with special needs is the lowest of the low. But, you'd be surprised at what I saw during my teaching tenure. Or…maybe you wouldn't.

Secondly, this response uses a touch of the Golden Rule. Whether they really are funny or not, the aggressor is getting a bit of an ego stroke while also being shown that their mean words have no effect.

Finally, your child is learning a valuable life lesson: how to process the mean words of someone else without taking offense, because, remember, they're just words. And as we said earlier, words only have the power that the listener gives them.

**Response number two:** *So?*

Let me just say, I love this one. It's probably my favorite. It's short. It's easy to memorize. It's EFFECTIVE!

In 1997, a book was published called *The Meanest Thing to Say,* by Bill Cosby. Yes, THAT Bill Cosby, the comedian. And, yes, I know about all the stuff in the news about him, but put that aside for a second and just focus on the lesson because it's a good one![50]

In the book, Little Bill and some friends at school play a game called "Playing the Dozens." Each person gets twelve chances to be mean to another person. Whoever says the meanest thing wins. As you can imagine, things started off light and funny, but quickly escalated until Little Bill's feelings got hurt and he became extremely angry. He was so mad, he couldn't concentrate on his homework that night. He had to prepare to settle the score and win the game the next day. Little Bill told his family about the game during dinner. His father, Big Bill, chimed in and taught him a simple response that was unbeatable: *So?*

Little Bill tried and tried but he could not top his dad. He kept getting met with, "So?" The more he tried, the more frustrated he got…and he started running out of mean things to say. Finally, he realized that nothing could top, "So?" It showed resilience and, ultimately, patience.

---

[50] Of course I'm not advocating or dismissing anything about the behavior he was accused of.

The next day, the game was on. Michael, Little Bill's opponent, began hurling insults at Little Bill.

"So?" Little Bill replied.

Michael tried another insult, worse than the first.

"So?" Little Bill answered.

Michael began to freak out! He was so frustrated that Little Bill wasn't getting upset and fighting back. He figured Little Bill would be in tears by this point. But, alas, Little Bill was actually laughing and kept responding with, "So?"

Eventually, Michael became frustrated and gave up. And then later on the two made up and became friends, blah blah blah… happily ever after.

I'm a big fan of the thinking that the best and most effective solutions are often the easiest to find. "So?" is that solution. Wanna know something cool? I've not only used, "So?" myself, but I've taught students to use it as well. It worked 100% of the time. It shows resilience. It leaves room for humor. It allows for emotional stability. It's easy to use and memorize. You can't top, "So?"

"So?" reminds me of a boy I knew in elementary school; Charlie. He was a good kid. Innocent, kind-hearted and super smart. A bit overweight and not very athletic. He had a lisp, which mirrored his father's. He was really into Star Trek, Star Wars, model planes and cub scouts. His innocent demeanor also allowed him to be easily upset-able. There were a few times where he would become upset and cry over seemingly small issues. By most standards, he was an easy target for the mean kids in school. Nobody ever really gave him a rough time, but, as kids will do, we all got into our fair share of name-calling and roasting matches in the name of fun and humor.

One day, Charlie became the target during one of these matches we were having.[51] How did he respond? He would say, "Prooooove it" while sounding like the pitches of a doorbell. The

---

[51] Yes, I was involved. Not proud of it. I was quick to learn the error of my ways.

result? We got tired of saying things to him. We got tired of hearing "Prooooove it" over and over. We moved on.

## *Here's My Card*

A friend of mine hands out "Peace Cards" that are the size of a business card. These cards contain short, effective and easy-to-use responses that anyone, any age, any ability can use to diffuse a situation. And they work! He told me a story of one boy who had learning differences, could not understand social cues, could not think of nor memorize any type of comeback; whether it was kind or not. After receiving a Peace Card, he kept it with him at all times, ready for action at a second's notice. One day it finally happened. Someone said something mean to him. He pulled out the card, read the first response and…it worked! The mean kid left him alone and never tried to insult him again. The boy walked a little taller from then on, knowing that he had the secret weapon to deal with mean people right in his pocket.

# KATRINA

A few years ago, I was privileged to be asked to visit eight schools in South Dakota within two days. It was a great, busy, and amazingly fun trip. The children's therapy organization that sponsored the programming for the area's schools was incredibly hospitable and really went above and beyond with scheduling everything.

During the second day, I was to visit five middle schools and perform a full student body assembly at each. The first assembly started at 8:30 AM and most of the rest of the day was a whirlwind. When we got to the last school, the students were already filing into the gym. There was probably close to 1,000 students from 6th through 8th grade. I could tell right away that this was going to be a fun group.

Towards the end of my assembly, I asked for a volunteer from the audience to play "Stop It" with me - in front of the whole school. I said, "I need a volunteer to come down here and make fun of me. Like...roast me!" Several hands went up, but I couldn't ignore this one young lady in the front middle section of the bleachers. Not only was she raising her hand, but there was about 30 other students around her pointing and egging me on to pick her. Usually, that means the volunteer is going to be a good one. Of course I chose her. As soon as I pointed at her, the entire gym either applauded or roared a collective, "Ooooooooo!" I knew I was in for a tough match.

The young lady was a seventh grader. Average height and blonde hair. She looked friendly. The principal's face turn pale. She looked terrified for me and for the fact that she was unsure of what would come out of this girl's mouth. I asked, "What's your name, my friend?"

"Shut up, loser," she snapped back into the microphone. The crowd erupted in laughter. I laughed, too.

"No, no. We're not playing just yet. I have to tell you the rules first. Geez, eager beaver!" In mid chuckle, I asked her name again.

"Katrina," she answered.

I explained the rules to the game, the crowd screamed "ACTION," and we were off. She was good. I mean, almost too good. Her insults were quick, funny and pushed the envelope. To be honest, it was hard not to laugh. She was hilarious, although I'd hate to be on the receiving end if she was legitimately coming after me. The more upset I acted, the meaner she would be. It was perfect. This went on for about a minute and a half when I stopped the game. The crowd understood the point. Katrina was hilarious and I could not stop her from being mean to me by responding negatively.

Then I said, "Ok, we're going to play again." All of the students cheered as if to say, "Alright, we get to see her roast him again!" The looks on the teachers' faces said, "Is he nuts? Why would he do this to himself? Didn't he learn his lesson from the first time?" The crowd screamed "ACTION," and round 2 was underway.

Now, the point of round 2 is to show how resilience and using the Golden Rule to respond to mean behavior can actually defuse a situation, calm the aggressor down, and make the law of reciprocity work in your favor. Usually, it only takes about 30 seconds for my volunteer to give up because they fall right into my trap. It is very difficult to stay mean to someone when they are being respectful, civil and kind in return. Not so with Katrina. She would not quit. I was kind. I paid her compliments. I was not getting upset. I was making jokes about myself. I was laughing at her insults. I was pulling out every trick I knew. SHE WOULD NOT QUIT! I thought I had met my match. This was taking forever! Eventually, I resorted to "So." Anything she said from then on, I just responded, "So." It was my last chance. My last resort.

Finally after about 30 seconds of "So," Katrina gave up. She said, "I'm done."

"What do you mean you're done?" I asked.

"I'm done. I'm bored. You're not reacting and it's not fun."

I grinned. "So, I win?!"

With a smart-aleck look, she said, "I guess."

Part of me was so relieved. I knew I would win. I just had to be more persistent than Katrina. Relentless, actually.

As the students were dismissing, the principal approached me with a huge smile. She said that Katrina was known as the meanest girl in school. "I believe it," I said with a laugh.

"No," she said. "You don't understand. She's always in my office for bullying and nothing works. We've tried detention, suspension, everything. But today, the entire school just watched you take down the meanest girl in school. Now every single student knows how to deal with her."

I was humbled. I didn't know that before going into it. All I did was keep calm in the face of adversity, respond how I wanted to be treated, and have patience.

Here's the lesson: If you want your child to win, they have to be persistent. No wavering. 100% every time. One slip up will send them back a step, possibly more. They'll have that much ground to make up. Some aggressors back down quicker than others. Just stay the course. It will work.

# PART 3: HELP!  MY KID IS A BULLY!

# THE CALL

Picture this:

It's a crazy day at work. You've been swamped all morning. Your boss asked you to stay late. You have work backing up faster than a toilet at Taco Bell. You finally get a second to look at the clock. 12:07. "Ahh, lunch time," you say to yourself. You go to the fridge, grab your lunch bag and head to the lunch room. You sit down, sigh, open your lunch and pull out the...oh! Phone's ringing. You know the number from somewhere but can't quite place it.

You: *Hello?*

Caller: *Hi, Mrs. Jones?*

You: *Yes?*

Caller: *Hi, this is Mrs. Jacobs at Great Ridge Middle School.*

You: *Mmhmm.* {As you chew that first delicious bite of ham sandwich that your stomach has been growling for.}

Caller: *We are having a bit of an issue with Benjamin here at school.*

You: *What do you mean? What's wrong?*

Caller: *Well, he's been bullying other students.*

You: *What?! When? How?!*

Caller: *It's been almost daily. Several students have come forward with accusations and we, as the school, need to take this seriously. So, Benjamin will be serving in-school suspension for three days, beginning tomorrow morning. We're hopeful that will correct his behavior.*

Hopefully, you've never had to take a phone call like that. Maybe you have. Maybe you didn't even get a phone call. I've heard of some schools just sending a note home or, even worse, just expecting the kid to communicate the issues. Either way, it's a rough situation.

First thing's first: Don't freak out. I know, easier said than done, especially when someone uses the big, bad "B" word in an accusatory way against your child. But, just pump the brakes for a second. Think about how things can go.

You could give the school a piece of your mind. Tell them how crazy they are, call the principal a few names, angrily plead your case right then and there, drive the wedge even further between the relationship of you and the school, and ultimately give the school a reason to think you are that crazy parent whose apple hasn't fallen far from the tree.[52]

You could figure out who the tattletale is and give their parents the same piece of your mind; thereby perpetuating the already escalated conflict and giving them another reason to post all kinds of crazy things about you on social media. After that, there's no telling how many people will know your business and chime in with their two cents. Still, nothing solved.

You could believe the school, let it stew all day and really let Junior have it when you get home, which wouldn't do much for your parent-child relationship. Or, you can try to figure out why and how things got to this point and find the best way to help your child stay away from a mess like this in the future, whether they are at fault or not.

Just so we're clear, I suggest the latter. There is no sense in adding to the already divisive, high-tension situation. As I've found,

---

[52] Trust me, there are many times where the "apple-tree" comparison is made.

many times, the biggest part of the "bullying" issue is actually how it is handled between the school and the parents. Let's not fall into this dangerous trap. The best way to get through this is to have both parties, school and parents, working together on the same page to take care of the whole situation, allowing everyone involved to save face and prevent future conflict.

Yes, you are upset, and you have a right to be. The very fact that someone has given your child such a label is almost a sense of bullying in and of itself, if you think about it. You're probably thinking things like, "They don't know my child." "It's not his fault. He was provoked." "She's not the only one who picks on other kids. It happens all over the school. Why is my kid singled out?" "None of the teachers like my kid. They're always out to get him." "The other kid picks on my kid, too. It's not a one-sided issue." And on and on and on. Again, keep calm. The more freaking out that happens, the worse things will get.

Your next step is to figure out why this came up as an issue. If your child has been accused of aggressive behavior, find out exactly what happened. Remember, define the specific behavior. The word "bully" and "bullying" are off limits to you.[53] Once you know exactly what happened, you can begin to learn why. Ask yourself, "What type of behavior is my child using that got him/her accused of bullying?" Chances are, it falls into one of the categories we discussed earlier in the Aggression Trifecta: humor, victimization and/or control. Here's what I mean.

If you learn that your child is making mean jokes about another student's weight, you know that he is using jokes and humor in a way that is being taken in a hurtful way. Or, if you find out that your child is angry, lashing out or trying to get some type of revenge against another student, you may have a victim on your hands. Or, let's say that your child is picking on, annoying, poking, pinching, teasing, bothering and tormenting others just for the simple fact of trying to feel like top dog; because it's just fun to watch someone else react and get upset. Dominance. Control.

---

[53] I feel like we're going to need that reminder a few times.

117

Maybe there are multiple things at play. It's common for a student to be using mean jokes in an effort to simply exert their control over someone else; or just because it's fun to watch them get upset. I've also seen students, who were having a rough day/week/life, use rude jokes to make someone else feel bad in order to deal with their negative feelings. That's all three in one situation! Regardless, when you can objectively look at the situation…calmly… you can identify what type of behavior(s) are being used. Once you do that, you can start to pull back the layers to figure out why they are doing it, how to help them, and, using everything in previous chapters, to make sure they don't get caught up in another situation like this again.

# HOW COULD YOU?!

### *Hurting People Hurt People*

You're probably wondering, "Why the heck is my child resorting to this behavior?" The simplest, and most common answer is this: over 90% of people that are labeled as "bullies" actually feel like a victim in some area of their life. Something in their life is not going as they think it should. It could be family issues, lack of true friends, academic problems, divorce, they feel wronged by someone, or that they simply just don't feel like they are being treated fairly. Perhaps they felt hurt or wronged by the person they decided to act out against. They're angry. They want retribution.

So what do they do? They may think that the way to get ahead is to put someone else down. They might find an escape in laughing at someone else's expense. They may be physically aggressive, using pushing, shoving and roughhousing to show their dominance.[54] They act out. They do things to compensate for the shortcomings in their life. They're hurting, so they hurt others.

Many times, especially in this scenario, punishing them because of their choice to act out is not the best way to handle things. If they already feel like a victim, they need some empathy. Yelling, screaming and punishing may actually do more harm than good. Yes, they need to understand that their behavior is not acceptable, but that comes after you get to the root cause of the situation. You need to have one of those talks and find out what is

---

[54] Non-criminal physical aggression.

hurting them. A heart-to-heart. What's bothering them? Do they feel wronged by something or someone? Do they feel as if they were acting in defense? Do they feel like they are being treated unfairly in some way? We'll talk more about proper discipline in a bit.

Often times in this situation, when you ask your child why they acted the way they did, they will respond with, "Well he did _____ to me first!" If you're a teacher or a parent with multiple kids, I bet you've heard that a million times. They feel justified in reciprocating the mean behavior because they feel like they are standing up for themselves in an attempt to win the domination battle; even though, as we discussed earlier, reciprocity only makes things worse. But, to them, at that moment, the only way they know how to deal with the negative hand they've been dealt is to take it out on someone else. Is it right? No. Am I defending it? No. So, why are they doing it? Because they need to be **taught** how to properly deal with their negative emotions.

If your child is feeling victimized in some way, I'd encourage you to go back and re-read the section on resilience. Chances are, your child may be thinking one or some of these following things:

*"I must perform well and receive approval from important people. Otherwise, I am a failure."*

*"Every person must treat me fairly and protect me from pain. Otherwise, they should be punished."*

*"Life must be comfortable and give me what I want. Otherwise, life is unbearable."*

Check out those statements. They are demands. **Must.** Fixed mindset demands. If they are holding any of those beliefs, they need to be helped. They need help turning their fixed, rigid thoughts into more flexible, growth oriented thoughts.

I'm sure you're probably thinking, "But, Chris, I've told him a million times…." I'm sure you have, but remember who and what you're dealing with: a child with a developing brain. Remember what it's like to be a teenager?[55]  As adults, our brains are, or should be, fully developed - including our reasoning and decision-making skills. Many studies show that those things are not fully developed until age 25.[56]  While that part of the brain is still developing, what do kids live on?  The amygdala - the emotional center.  Fight or flight.  Instant reaction.  That's why kids, especially teenagers, are so emotional.  If they are feeling victimized, you better believe that emotional side of the brain is going to show its face.  It's how we're all wired.  Can kids control it?  Yes.  Is it difficult?  Extremely.  Can they do it?  Absolutely, but it takes practice.

In a bit, we're going to talk about coping skills, which will be beneficial if your child feels victimized and has been accused of being a "bully."  Most mental health professionals would suggest helping your child find ways to cope with the negative situations that are triggering them to lash out.  Coping skills will help them deal with whatever situation is making them feel like a victim.

## Comedians

As we saw earlier, humor is one mode of aggressive behavior. Laughing at something's or someone's expense is the very definition of humor.  The funniest jokes are often those that have the biggest "butts" and/or get as close as possible to the offensive line without crossing it.  It is important to note, however, that once the line is crossed, the humor suffers, and often fails.  You know what I mean. There are some jokes that are hilarious because they ride that line. But, then there are some jokes that are just distasteful, cruel and over the line.  I've seen many comics absolutely bomb on stage because they didn't know the limit.  Which brings me to my point:

**Know the limits.**

I'm reminded of a female standup comedian who, for a number of years, was huge in the comedy world.  Movies, TV

---

[55] My awesome wife constantly reminds me that I think and act like one on a regular basis.

[56] I'm going to say that's an average, because we all know that one person who acts more like an animal than a person.

specials, awards, you name it. She was at the height of her career. But, it was easy to tell that something was changing in her. She was becoming more flippant, vulgar and offensive as time went on. Then it happened. She got her own Netflix special. It was pumped up for weeks! Much of the country was excited! The day came. Her special dropped on Netflix and…it tanked! It got to the point that, within the first 48 hours, Netflix had to suspend the "comments" and "feedback" features on the site because of all of the negative backlash from this one comedy special.

What happened? She was over-the-top! Vulgarity - language and subject matter. Filthy, raunchy, disgusting. Just…ugh! She didn't know her audience. She didn't know the limits. And, to my knowledge, she has not done another standup comedy special since then; for Netflix or anyone else.

If your child is accused of "bullying" because they are making rude jokes about another student, they may be doing it because they think they are being funny. And I get it! Laughter is addictive. It's affirming. If you're getting laughs, you want to keep getting them, sometimes regardless of who the joke's target is. But, it's important to know the line, or at least be able to understand when they are getting close to it. While it's important for the "butts" of the jokes to practice and build resilience to protect and control their own emotions, it's equally important for the comedian to understand their audience and know how far to go with the jokes. Obviously, when feelings are hurt, it's too far. If there are tears, stop. When these kids are confronted about the inappropriateness of their behavior, they usually respond with, "I was just kidding." Whether it's true or not, they must understand limits.

### *Mission: Control*

Now, I'm not ridiculous. I know that sometimes kids make jokes, spread rumors and engage in certain behaviors to hurt others on purpose. I can't tell you how many times I've seen a group of 3 or 4 kids gathered around a single student poking fun at his weight, appearance, etc. Every time, the student was noticeably upset, but the aggressors just kept on tormenting. They were having fun watching the student get upset. No other reason. Just plain being mean. They enjoyed watching their target get upset. It was fun for them to watch the student get upset. They felt like winners by making someone else feel like a loser.

Believe it or not, this type of behavior is actually very telling of someone who has strong leadership qualities.

**Hold up...*WHAT?!***

I know it sounds weird. Let me explain.

### *My Kid's a What?*

Many times, kids that are labeled as "bullies" are actually great leaders. I know it sounds crazy, but if you think about it, bullying behavior is actually a form of leadership. Now, no *good* leader would act in a negatively aggressive way towards their subordinates. But, leadership in and of itself is all about influence. Leaders are put in place to influence others. A great leader can positively influence others to accomplish amazing things - good and bad. Coercion, manipulation and dominance are all types of behaviors used in attempts to influence others to do things.

Leaders want respect. The most common mistake made, however, is that one can dominate, manipulate or coerce respect out of someone by putting them down. True respect is earned. Respect given out of fear is not true respect. It is thrall. I can't tell you how many alleged "bullies" I have spoken with who have told me they want to be respected. They want to be the top dog. And they think the way to do it is to take it by force. Remember the "King of the Mountain" example from earlier? Your child wants to be king, or queen, of the mountain and they think the way to do it is to push everyone else down.

Is your child exhibiting natural leadership qualities? Do they show a high level of competency in certain areas? I'm willing to bet they do. Someone who displays a great deal of competency is primed for leadership. They are just missing one other piece: character. Character, in this case, includes one's ability to create and develop good relationships with others. Once competency and character are in place, that leader is unstoppable.

Think of it this way: Professional basketball is an amazing breeding ground for leaders - good and bad. I think Michael Jordan is the greatest player of all time. Not only was he competent, but he had an amazing level of character. The result? He will go down in history as one of the greatest players and leaders in the NBA. Imagine if *all* professional athletes played and acted like M.J. I doubt you'd hear much about scandals, cheating and the "cry baby" culture that is rearing its head into the world of pro sports.

Some often argue the case that there are other players, especially in recent years, that are better than Jordan. While I agree that there are some players that may be more skilled and dominant on the court, they lack greatly in the character department. Do they still get the ball? Yes. Do people still count on them to win the game? Yes. Do they get a fair amount of respect? Yes. Are they seen as leaders on their team? Sure. Do we want our kids looking up to them? No.

Character is huge. Your child may be able to accomplish something. Your child may be able to influence others. But, are they doing it properly? Chances are, if your child is being labeled as a "bully," they are showing great competency in certain areas of their life, they just need to work on their character a bit. Reign it in. Use it in a positive way. They have a natural ability to dominate. They're great at being able to influence others. Their presence commands attention and respect when they enter a room. They have a knack for getting others to do and feel things as *they* dictate. If the subordinates act accordingly, they are rewarded, included in the cool group; or at least left alone. If they don't, they are treated in a negative way.

Encourage your child to find and use good leadership qualities - building others up, empowerment and empathy rather than negative methods like threats, coercion and manipulation. They'll find that they'll have more respect, more real friends and more opportunities for true leadership that makes a difference. I've challenged several parents of "bullies" to find them an opportunity to lead. Find something they're good at. Then, find a way for them to lead. Give them the power they want, in a controlled environment, so they can learn the magic of empowering others using positive leadership qualities.

124

## _Darcy_

During an upper elementary school assembly in central Nebraska, I met a 6th grade young lady named Darcy. She sat in the top row of the bleachers with her eyes locked on me the entire time I was speaking. She barely cracked a smile at any of my jokes and remained almost completely stoic the entire time. As I spoke, I felt myself operating on autopilot while my mind wondered so many things. Who was she? Was she just not amused by me? Did she not care what I was saying? Was she tired? Did she get in trouble before the assembly? Was she just having a bad day? Every other kid was laughing and tracking with me, so what was her deal?

Towards the end of my assembly program, I usually seek a volunteer from the audience to come up and play "Stop It," which is described in detail in the appendix. In the game, they get to make fun of me while I illustrate how someone's anger and retaliation during a conflict can escalate the situation and make it worse. Then I show them how responding in respect and kindness can dissolve the conflict. So, at this school, I asked for a volunteer from the audience to come down and roast me. Darcy timidly rose her hand. As soon as she did, however, every student in the bleachers began pointing to her and begging me to pick her. I pointed at her and said, "My lady in the black jacket, come on down." The rest of the students erupted in applause. The principal peered over from the side of the bleachers, became wide-eyed and began cheering just as loud as the kids. As Darcy made her way down from the bleachers, I knew this was going to be good.

"What's your name?" I asked.

"Darcy," she answered. She pushed her long brown hair behind her shoulder.

"Ok, Darcy we're going to play a game. When I say action, you call me an idiot. Can you do that?" What she said next shook me to my core.

"Yeah." She looked down at her black, horse riding-style boots. "My dad says mean things all the time, so I'm used to hearing things like that." I went to pull the microphone away from her face, but she continued. "The other night, he got so mad he punched a hole in the door." I didn't want make a big deal of it right then in front of the whole school, so I just continued with the game; knowing I'd have to find her later.

The game couldn't have gone better. In round one, she did a great job being mean to me and really made a great show for the student body as I kept acting upset and defensive. She was theatrical, bold and full of charisma. In round 2, she was stumped with my kindness in response to her insults. She gave up.[57]

I finished the assembly, gave the microphone back to the principal and she dismissed the students. As the teachers were directing their kids out of the bleachers, I walked over to the principal and said, "So...Darcy. Her story...umm..."

The principal interrupted, "Oh yes. She has so many problems at home. Dad is in and out of jail. Mom is verbally abusive. No stability. She's the school tough girl. She's really the only one that gives us any problems. That's why everyone was excited to see how she would do in your game. But, to me, that just means she needs more love while she's here. All the kids kind of give her space when she needs it. I just wish I knew how to do more for her."

"I can tell you my opinion," I said. She looked at me with hope in her eyes. "Put her on your student council. She's a natural leader. She just has to learn how to hone her strong personality and leadership qualities in the right direction."

"Of course! She'd be perfect," the principal said happily. "All the kids look up to her anyway. It'll be such a positive thing in her life."

Just then, Darcy walked by with her class. I called her over and asked for a hug. She wrapped her arms around my waist and I wrapped mine around her neck. I said, "Hey, friend. If nobody else tells you today, I love you." She looked at me as if she hadn't heard those words in ages.

---

[57] That's how it's supposed to go, by the way.

"We all love her," the principal said happily.

Darcy is a classic example of how all three parts of the Aggression Trifecta (humor, dominance and victimization) can come into play. She often used mean jokes, teasing, roughhousing and other aggressive behaviors to exert her dominance over others because she felt like a victim due to the fact that she had such a rough home life. She didn't trust many people, especially adults. The adults she *did* trust had to work extra hard to earn that trust, show incredible patience, play the "give and take" games, and really search themselves for love as they worked with such a child. The principal, a 30 year veteran of education, knew exactly what to do on day one. She knew it wasn't going to be easy, but she knew how to break Darcy's walls down and, not only get the teachers to love her, but the students, too. And it absolutely showed. When the love is so loud, nothing else can break through. The next step was to direct Darcy's leadership qualities in a positive way so that she could take that next step of owning her own life and truly becoming that strong, resilient kid who will, one day I'm sure, change the world.

### *Under Pressure*

There are some cases, of course, where your child may have been influenced by the wrong crowd. Maybe one, or some, of their friends have decided to engage in teasing, joking, taunting or gossiping about another student and your child gets sucked into it. Peer pressure. A desire to avoid being excluded.

Educational psychologist Dr. Michele Borba suggests that you get perspective about your own children from other people who are with your child on a regular basis. Their teachers, for example, are a great resource for understanding what your child is doing when they are not around you. Or, in another perspective, you can also tell a lot about your own children by the people they hang out with. A very wise and wealthy man once taught me that association is one of the greatest indicators of future success. He said, "Show me the five people you spend the most time with and I'll show you where you'll end up in ten years." As a parent, you need to understand who your child is spending time with. What you see may be eye-opening.

Some say, "Oh come on. I know my kid better than anyone. They know better. They don't do anything like that. They don't give in to the peer pressure of others. They know to be a good up-standing bystander."

Get ready. I'm going to drop a truth bomb. You may not like it, but it's often true. Ready? **Kids act differently around their parents.** Shocked? You shouldn't be. Don't lie. You know, as a kid, you put on an act for your parents from time to time to make it look like you were an innocent soul.

Now that I've twinged that nerve, let me go for the gold. (Honestly, though, if you haven't shut the book and sent me a nasty email by this point, I think you'll be ok.) **Kids don't always do what they're told.** I know I didn't. I'm an "adult" now, and I still don't. My wife will attest to that. You can teach, tell, rehearse, bribe...whatever. The fact is that every now and then, kids have a lapse in judgement and get mixed up in the wrong crowd at the wrong moment. Wrong place, wrong time. Even if you know that they know right from wrong, it will happen. No, that doesn't make it right. But, it happens. Again, look at things through the eyes of your pre-teen or teenage self. Were there ever times that you were engaged in something just because of who you hung out with? I know many adults who still find themselves in those situations. When in Rome, right?

If that's the case for your child, encourage them to deeply consider their social circle. Ask your child to weigh the pros and cons of spending time with certain people. Figure out if this was this just a one time thing or if it happens often. Consider what type of other decisions those people regularly make? Ask your child, "Can you trust that they won't treat *you* poorly if you don't conform to their ways in the future?" Encourage your child to use caution. They may need to upgrade their association. (Notice I said "encourage." I didn't say "demand" or "force." There's a huge difference.)

# RESTORE - DON'T DESTROY

We've all probably said or thought, "If my kid ever bullies another kid, they won't be able to sit down for a week." I get it. We don't want our kids to carry the label of "bully." More importantly, we want our kids to treat others with respect. After all, the sooner they learn it, the better off they'll be. So, we naturally resort to the simplest and easiest forms of punishment we know: a good ol' fashioned butt whoopin'. If you're not the spanking type, then you may want to go straight to grounding, taking away privileges and possessions, or extra chores.

There are many schools of thought about how to discipline children who engage in aggressive social behavior. Some like to invoke a zero tolerance or "one and done" policy. Screw up once and the punishments rain down. Others operate on a 3 strike protocol. Three strikes and you're out. This carries some benefit because it forces the child to consider consequences and motivate them to make better decisions. However, considering the developing brain, children will often feel as if they are being watched and under judgement of their past mistakes. In addition, they may also feel as if they are being set up to fail. There is another way, however. A new approach to disciplining children is making waves in schools and even prisons all over the country. It's called restorative justice, or restorative discipline.

People care a lot about how they're treated when they are punished; especially kids. It's easier for them to fixate on the *type* of punishment they experience rather than how their behavior may effect others. If they feel unfairly or aggressively treated in the punishment, they will show resentment toward authority and usually toward their target as well. Resentment turns into resistance, and resistance turns into disassociation and more aggression toward others. I once saw a video on social media of a father who made his "bully" son run home from school in the rain while the father followed behind in the car. Did the kid learn a lesson? I'm sure he did. But, at what price? What did that punishment ultimately do to that father/son relationship?

Restorative discipline practices take incidents that would usually result in punishment and create opportunities for students to become aware of the impact of their behavior, understand their obligation to take responsibility for their actions, and take steps to make things right; the ultimate display of empathy.[58] Through this process, students learn how to interact and manage their relationships with adults and peers. They become better equipped to understand how their actions impact others and how to monitor future behavior.

I like to think of it like this: they are learning their lesson, but learning it in a way where they get the help they need to prevent it from happening again. Dignity is preserved and relationships (student/student and student/adult) are kept in tact. I've seen restorative discipline work wonders for all parties involved. Check and make sure that your child's school is using restorative discipline processes. Trust me, it's an amazing tactic that works!

### *If Worse Comes to Worse*

Maybe you've tried everything. You're at your wits end. You're fed up. You've tried to reason with your child. You've tried punishments. It seems as if nothing is working. There is another option. If worse comes to worse, it's ok to consider professional counseling. I know, I know. Therapy carries a certain stigma: You're a bad parent. You've lost all control. Your kid is a bad kid. How can some stranger get to the bottom of things with *your* kid? They don't know your child like you do.

Trust me, I know. But, if anything, taking your child to counseling is a very beneficial thing that shows great strength on your part as a parent. Counselors have a way of getting people to open

---

[58] Isn't that how we want our kids to turn out anyway?

up, analyzing, and finding real solutions while preserving everyone's dignity. You want the best for your child, that's a given. It doesn't mean you're a bad parent or that you've lost control. It means that you are willing to do anything for your child.

Likely, there will be great focus on empathy; something that is greatly missing from many people today. Empathy will allow your child to understand the thoughts, feelings and emotions of others from the other's point of view. It's different than sympathy. Sympathy is seeing someone's feelings and emotions through your own lens. Empathy actually requires that you step outside of yourself and experience various parts of life through someone else's vantage point.

Want to know something cool? In order to gain empathy, you have to understand yourself, too. It's impossible to meet the needs of others if your needs aren't met. So, in the process of learning to be empathetic, your child will also learn more and more about themselves - why they are acting the way they are and how to control it. The ultimate result will be a child who is more compassionate, understanding, level-headed and empathetic which will serve him well for the rest of his life.

PART 4: SOMETHING FOR EVERYONE

# FROM MOPE TO COPE TO HOPE

We got a pressure cooker for Christmas recently. I love that thing. It's the one that's been advertised everywhere. People had been posting about it on social media, sharing recipes and uploading pictures of some amazing looking food. We were so excited to get one. But, there was one problem: I had never used a pressure cooker before. I didn't know how it worked; especially the steam pressure release valve.

My first attempted meal was something simple: chicken. Believe it or not, I actually read the directions. I poured in some water, put in the frozen chicken, seasoned it, put on the lid, pushed the right buttons and waited. It was easy. Set it and forget it. 20 minutes later, the cooker beeped and it was time to behold my creation. The directions said to perform a "slow release." As I looked all over the cooker, I whispered to myself, "Slow release... slow release.... Where's the 'slow release' button?" While I was looking for this nonexistent button, my elbow bumped the pressure release valve. I kid you not, a geyser of steam erupted from this thing that scared me so badly I literally fell down! I had two initial thoughts. First, do I still have a face? Second, how much pressure was in there for it to almost take my face off?

Coping skills are crucial for any and everyone who deals with stress in their life. So...everyone! Think of your emotions as a pressure cooker. If you don't know how to slowly release that pressure, one day that valve is going to blow. And when it does, it could be dangerous. You could explode or implode. It could mean harm to yourself or somebody else. Like a rubber band, if you are constantly stretched and stretched, with no relief, you will snap. And, if you've ever seen a rubber band snap, someone always has a tendency to get hurt.

People tend to hear the phrase "coping skills" and jump to thoughts of seeing a shrink and going through therapy. Trust me when I say that could not be further from the truth. It's not *just* for people who have gone through trauma or hard times. Everyone needs coping skills. They help you process through stress and pain. My friend, Jeff Veley, describes coping skills as "how you deal with how you feel." Teaching children how to cope with their emotions is crucial when it comes to dealing with the negative behavior of others. It's an incredible way to build resilience!

### *Hazardous to Your Health*

We all have stress: mental, physical and emotional. We all have pain: mental, physical and emotional. We all have things in life that we need to deal with. We all have difficult people in our lives that we need to deal with. And, we all have our ways of dealing with those things. We all need an escape sometimes. We all need to release that pressure. Unfortunately, some of those methods are unhealthy. By default, if you are not coping in a healthy manner, you are coping in an unhealthy one.

Unhealthy coping mechanisms often include things like:

- Drinking alcohol
- Smoking
- Using drugs
- Self-harm (cutting, burning, pulling out hair, tattooing, piercing, etc.)
- Drinking too much caffeine
- Spending money in excess
- Binge eating
- Refusing to eat/anorexia
- Bulimia
- Hitting/breaking things
- Sexual behaviors
- Avoiding the problem
- Making rash decisions

- Sleeping too much

This by no means is an exhaustive list, but it definitely covers the most common ones. If your child is exhibiting any of these behaviors, they may be trying to deal with something in their life. As a parent, it's up to you to help them.

## *Healthier Options*

I love looking at restaurant menus these days. It's kind of funny how they're laid out. The first couple of pages are usually the alcohol. Next, the appetizers. Right under the appetizers, in a small section, are the salads. Then come all of the normal foods - steaks, burgers, sandwiches, sides, and desserts. Then, on the last page, are the healthy options. All of the meals under 500 calories. Fat free. I've even been in restaurants where you have to ask for a special separate menu for the healthier options. Regardless, the healthy options on the menu are not always the most visible. They make it so easy to choose the unhealthy food. You have to do some digging if you want the stuff that can be good for you.

Healthy coping skills are the same way. They're not always the easiest things to do. Many times, it requires you to step back and think about the best way to deal with the stress and pain of a situation. Sure, all of the ones in the unhealthy category may be easier, more fun, more accessible, better tasting, or more comfortable. But, they are worse for you in the long run. Choosing the best healthy coping skills can actually help you overcome a multitude of issues in life. And helping your child discover, try out and refine healthy ways to cope can be a lifelong lesson that will serve them well forever.

Here are some healthy ways to deal with stress and negative situations:

- Deep breathing exercises
- Color - I actually used to laugh about adults needing to color until I tried it. It totally works!
- Rub your hands together - This actually works very well with over 80% of kids. It's also a natural soothing

mechanism used by babies in the womb. Use some hand lotion to enhance the sensations.
- Positive self-talk/Read positive, reaffirming statements - Nobody talks to you more than you. Your thoughts become your words. Words become actions. Actions become habits. Habits become character. Character becomes your destiny.
- Exercise/Take a walk - Studies show this is actually more effective and beneficial than anti-depressant medications.
- Prayer/Meditation
- Read
- Use calming essential oils
- Take a bath/shower
- Do something to help someone else - It's amazing how helping someone else can lift your own spirits.
- Play a game - Limited electronic use is ok here. But, be careful. It could turn into something unhealthy.
- Do a puzzle
- Play sports
- Play a musical instrument
- Watch a funny movie
- Hang out with a good friend who makes good decisions
- Listen to music/calming sounds/ASMR

I could go on, but hopefully you get the point. All of those things are calming, beneficial ways to deal with stress. Not only do they calm, but many of them also enhance other areas of life and, dare I say, help you learn new things.

It is important to note that there are some coping mechanisms that can be done "in the moment," and some that can't. For example, if your child is sitting in class trying to deal with a stressful situation, it is not feasible for them to go outside and kick a soccer ball, bang on a drum set or start doing a puzzle. However, they can breathe deeply and slowly. They can rub their hands together. They can excuse themselves from class for a moment to go to the restroom or get a drink. They can get through the moment until they are able to get to their favorite strategy. Help your child figure out what works for them in the moment *and* when they have some alone time. Different environments call for different strategies. Make sure you and your child understand the triggers, symptoms and appropriate responses in all of those environments.

## But What If...

Many times, students ask me, "But what if I can't think of anything to do. I'm not good at anything." My response to them is, "If you weren't at school, what would you be doing? If you had a day of free time, what would you do?" Whatever they say, as long as it is healthy and not detrimental, I encourage them to do that.

"But Chris," they say, "sometimes I'm so down I don't *want* to do anything."

I totally get it! I've been there. Sometimes, life is just super heavy and all you want to do is lay around and wallow in your pool of blah. Honestly, that's ok for a short time. But after that I'd say, "But you want to feel better, right? You don't want to *stay* in your angry/sad/negative frame of mind, do you?" (No matter what they say, the answer is always no.)

Understand this: the easiest way to change your feelings is by taking action. Feelings follow actions, not the other way around. If you waited to do something until you felt like it, especially when under great pressure and stress, it would never get done. If you want to change your feelings and emotions during a stressful situation, you have to act on it. The longer you wait, the harder it is to start. You may need to force yourself, or have a close friend or family member, also known as an accountability partner, force you.

## It's a Journey

Any way you want it, don't stop believing. Be good to yourself, faithfully.[59]

Sorry. I had to throw in some dad jokes. Anyway...

Jeff Veley made a great statement about coping skills during one of my podcast episodes. He said that coping skills and learning to deal with stress are not always just switches you can flip. It's a journey. He likened it to a road trip. You have to take breaks. You need to rest, refuel, make some U-turns, and get some help along the

---

[59] Those are all Journey songs, by the way.

way. "It's not a task to accomplish, it's a journey to take. So, give yourself some grace." Help your child discover, cultivate, develop and practice positive, healthy coping skills, no matter what side of the "bullying" problem they're on.

Use these steps on the coping journey:

1. Acknowledge the problem
2. Realize what you can and can't control
3. Focus on what you can control
4. Find healthy ways to cope in the moment and long term
5. Find ways to distance yourself from the stress if possible

# STOP USING THE "B" WORD

If I can ask one more thing before we wrap things up here, please do me and the rest of the world a favor. Let's retire the word "bully." Actually, let's bury it. I know I'm the "bully guy." I know it's what I do. I know it's how everyone knows how to describe the behaviors. I know it's a simple, catch-all term. It's so easy to use. I know I've used it several times throughout this book. I hope you understand why I did, though. I hope you understand that when I did, it was at strategic, carefully chosen times.

But, please, if you really want to stop "bullying," stop using the word. Using it will only give it life. It will give life to the word, the behavior, the fear, the anger, the clouded judgement…everything we're trying to get rid of.

The University of Texas in Arlington conducted a study which showed that schools that have strict anti-bullying policies in place actually have higher "bullying" numbers.[60] Why is that? Why are they counter-productive? It's simple, really.

If you look at how the definition of "bullying" has been packaged and sold, plus what kids are generally being taught (or not taught) in school about how to handle mean behavior, plus a decrease in people's resilience, plus the lack of training that teachers and staff actually get on the subject, plus the constant overuse of the word, you have a recipe for disaster.

---

[60] https://www.uta.edu/news/releases/2013/09/jeong-bullying.php

139

Kids are believing that "bullying" is something as small as sticking their tongue out and making faces all the way up to the Holocaust.[61] They are told to report any and all mean behavior. So, they do! And now, they're reporting it at a rate that has never been seen before. The result? All of the mean behaviors are taken personally, blown up and documented as "bullying" incidents. So, it's easy to think that things are getting worse.

### Stop using the big, bad "B" word!

The lack of resilience in people everywhere is astounding. All you have to do is turn on the TV for two minutes and it becomes evident that people (adults and children alike) are offended much easier than ever before. Unfortunately, that is spilling over into our children and in our schools. They don't know how to handle the negativity of life, including the mean behavior of others. Obviously, I'm not talking about everyone, but I'm sure you can think of at least one person who fits this profile.

Don't freak out, though. I can't tell you how many teachers, counselors and administrators that I have talked to that have all told me the same thing in more or less words: "There is no bullying problem. There's a resilience problem."

Please, take everything I've divulged in here and use it. Use it to help your child. Use it to change the climate of your child's school. Use it to change how you do things in your home. And, if you're a school worker, use it to change your school's culture.

We all want the same thing for the next generation. We don't want them to be affected by mean words, rude jokes, non-criminal physical aggression, rumors, exclusion, etc. We want them to be able to handle their own social problems. We want them to be resilient. We want them to be empathetic. We want them to live by the Golden Rule. We want them to believe in themselves. We want them to be empowered. We're not going to get there by doing the same old things that aren't working.

---

[61] Yes, I know of a teacher who told that to her students.

Change is a powerful thing. Powerful but difficult. Difficult but necessary. If you want things to turn out differently, embrace the change. Be willing to try something different. Embrace resilience. Embrace the Golden Rule. Embrace empathy. Above all, embrace the next generation.

# APPENDIX
## STOP IT!

Here's a little game to help kids practice and reinforce how to deal with mean people. One person is the "aggressor" and one is the "target." (If this is your first couple times playing, the adult should be the "target" and the child should be the "aggressor.")

In Round 1, the "aggressor" begins by calling the "target" a name. The "target" should respond to the insult by getting upset, pretending to cry, making a fuss, calling the "aggressor" names in return, etc.

Example:

Aggressor: *You're an idiot.*

Target: *Stop it! You're hurting my feelings! I'm telling!*

Aggressor: *So what, idiot!*

Target: *You're always so mean! Leave me alone.*

Aggressor: *What are you going to do, cry baby?*

Continue in the manner as the conflict escalates until it is clear that the conflict cannot be resolved in this manner.

In Round 2, keep the same roles, except, this time, the "target" should remain calm, refrain from getting upset and respond with kind words, humor and other non-threatening means.

Example:

Aggressor: *You're an idiot.*

Target: *Yeah, sometimes I do silly things. But, we all do.*

Aggressor: *You sure do, idiot.*

Target: *If it makes you happy calling me an idiot, that's fine. I don't have any problem with you, though.*

Continue in this manner and watch the conflict fizzle out.

After playing, discuss the difference between the two situations. Which one gave the better results and why?

Some things to consider:

1. Make sure all participants understand and follow the guidelines for appropriate language in your setting.

2. This is an educational game. It may be necessary for the adult to be the "target" for the first number of sessions. If at any time things seem like they are getting close to being out of hand, stop the game right away.

3. Once you are confident that your child is ready, play Round 3 in which they become the "target" and must use their newfound skills to shut you, the aggressor, down.

# ABOUT THE AUTHOR

Chris "Shoof" Scheufele is an author, speaker, musician and educator with over a decade of experience in the classroom. His entertaining and educational programs have been recognized by schools nationwide, earning him a teacher of the year award in 2017. He enjoys traveling, cooking, sleeping and playing with his kids. A native of Baltimore, Maryland, he currently lives in Nebraska with his wife and children.

www.ChrisInTheClassroom.com

Made in the USA
Columbia, SC
26 August 2022